Prop

Mrs. H. U. Dortmund
1172 Pennsylvania ave
Columbus, O.

KINGDOM SERIES

VOL. 2

Christ's Second Coming
and
What Will Follow

BY

H. M. RIGGLE

GOSPEL TRUMPET COMPANY
ANDERSON, IND.

Copyright, 1918,

BY

GOSPEL TRUMPET COMPANY

BY THE SAME AUTHOR

CONTENTS

Jesus Is Coming Again

It is an undeniable fact that the church in her present condition is instructed to look for the return of Christ from heaven as the next great event. Nowhere are we instructed to look for a pre- or post-millennium. During his earthly ministry, Christ was careful to inform his disciples of his departure from them. But he also taught them, "I WILL COME AGAIN" (John 14:3). Yes, the same Christ who once trod the shores of Galilee; who traveled over the Judean hills, ministering salvation to hungry souls and healing to all those who were oppressed of the devil, is coming again. To the disciples who stood gazing into heaven at the time of Christ's ascension, the angels announced, "This same Jesus, which is taken up from you into heaven, shall so come in like manner as ye have seen him go into heaven" (Acts 1:11). Paul

confirms this truth by boldly declaring
that "unto them that look for him shall
he appear **the second time**" (Heb. 9:
28). James adds this testimony: "The
coming of the Lord draweth nigh"
(Jas. 5: 8).

THIS SECOND COMING IS NOT MERELY HIS
SPIRITUAL PRESENCE

That Christ promised his disciples
that he would return to them in the person and presence of the Holy Spirit, we
do not deny. He said, "I will not leave
you comfortless: I will come to you."
In connection with this promise, he said,
"I will pray the Father, and he shall
give you another Comforter, that he
may abide with you forever; even the
Spirit of truth; whom the world can not
receive." "At that day ye shall know
that I am in my Father, and ye in me,
and I in you." "If a man love me, he
will keep my words: and my Father will
love him, and we will come unto him,

and make our abode with him" (John 14: 16, 17, 20, 23). He further promised, "I will never leave thee, nor forsake thee"; and "I will be with you alway, even unto the end of the world." "That Christ may dwell in your hearts by faith." These texts, with many others that we might cite, clearly show Christ's spiritual presence with his church during the present dispensation. But this must not be confounded with his personal coming at the end of this age. "When the Son of man shall come in his glory, and all his holy angels with him, then shall he sit upon the throne of his glory: and before him shall be gathered all nations" (Matt. 25:31, 32).

But One Personal Coming of Christ Future

"What shall be the sign of thy coming?" (Matt. 24: 3). "Now we beseech you, brethren, by the coming of our Lord Jesus Christ" (2 Thess. 2: 1). "I pray God your whole spirit and soul and body be preserved blameless unto the coming of our Lord Jesus Christ" (1 Thess. 5: 23). "Whom the Lord shall . . . destroy with the brightness of his coming" (2 Thess. 2: 8). "Looking for that blessed hope, and the glorious appearing of the great God and our Savior Jesus Christ" (Tit. 2: 13). "And now, little children, abide in him; that, when he shall appear, we may have confidence, and not be ashamed before him at his coming" (1 John 2: 28). "Be patient therefore, brethren, unto the coming of the Lord. . . . Be ye also patient: stablish your hearts; for the coming of the Lord draweth nigh" (Jas. 5: 7, 8).

Some latter-day teachers advocate three comings of the Lord yet future, but all the foregoing scriptures, and many more, teach us to look for but one

coming, which will be at the end of this
world. "Christ was once offered to bear
the sins of many; and unto them that
look for him shall he appear the **second**
time" (Heb. 9:28). This text is decisive. It teaches but two advents of
Christ to this world. His first advent
was in the beginning of this age, when,
as a Savior, he was offered to bear the
sins of many; and his second appearing
will be at the end of the Christian era.
Note the language—"He will appear **the
second time."** Not a second, third,
and fourth time, but just the second
time. There is only one personal coming of Christ future.

IT WILL BE COINCIDENT WITH THE END OF THE WORLD

After Jesus told the disciples of the
destruction of the temple, they asked
him the important question, "What
shall be the sign of thy coming, and of
the end of the world?" (Matt. 24:3).

The disciples understood that when
Christ would come again, this world
would come to an end. In answering
this question, Jesus said, "And this gospel of the kingdom shall be preached
in all the world for a witness unto all
nations; and then shall the end come"
(Matt. 24: 14). Peter informs us that
"the end of all things is at hand"; that
is, soon to appear. And this includes
the world on which we live. It also com-
prehends all things pertaining to Time,
the end of probation, the end of salvation opportunities, the end of all earthly
things. "But the day of the Lord will
come as a thief in the night; in the
which the heavens will pass away with
a great noise, and the elements shall
melt with fervent heat, the earth also
and the works that are therein shall be
burned up" (2 Pet. 3: 10).

IT WILL BE VISIBLE

"And when he had spoken these

things, while they beheld, he was taken up; and a cloud received him out of their sight. And while they looked stedfastly toward heaven as he went up, behold, two men stood by them in white apparel; which also said, Ye men of Galilee, why stand ye gazing up into heaven? this same Jesus, which was taken up from you into heaven, shall so come in like manner as ye have seen him go into heaven" (Acts 1: 9-11). This is clear. "This same Jesus" shall come again, **"in like manner"** as he went up. He went up bodily and visibly. It was a personal ascension of Christ into heaven. They saw him ascend—"a cloud received him out of their sight." "In like manner" shall he descend from heaven. Language could not be framed to more clearly teach Christ's second advent as a personal, visible coming. "Behold, he cometh with clouds; and **every eye shall see him,** and they also which pierced him: and all kindreds of

the earth shall wail because of him"
(Rev. 1: 7). "The powers of heaven
shall be shaken. And then shall they
see the Son of man coming in a cloud
with power and great glory" (Luke 21:
26, 27). "Then **shall they see** the Son
of man coming in the clouds with great
power and glory" (Mark 13: 26). "And
then shall appear the sign of the Son of
man in heaven: and then shall all the
tribes of the earth mourn, and they shall
see the Son of man coming in the clouds
of heaven with power and great glory"
(Matt. 24: 30). "Ye shall see the Son
of man sitting on the right hand of
power, and coming in the clouds of
heaven" (Mark 14: 62).

A number of millennial advocates
teach that Christ has already come in
his second advent. But this modern
"presence of Christ" theory is without
the support of a single text of Scripture.
The positive testimony is that when he
comes in the clouds of heaven, "every

shall it come on all them that dwell on
the face of the whole earth. Watch ye
therefore, and pray always, that ye may
be accounted worthy to escape all these
things that shall come to pass, and to
stand before the Son of man" (Luke
21: 34-36). "But as the days of Noe
were, so shall the coming of the Son of
man be. For as in the days that were
before the flood they were eating and
drinking, marrying and giving in marriage, until the day that Noe entered
into the ark, and knew not until the
flood came, and took them all away; so
shall also the coming of the Son of man
be" (Matt. 24: 37-39).

This is very plain. The coming of
Christ is a great and solemn event pending, for which the church is to look and
watch and be ready. The day and hour
of his coming the Father only knoweth.
When the rending heavens shall reveal
his presence, this world will be in a
Sodom state, and as the antediluvian

eye shall see him"; not only the righ
eous, but all the tribes of the eart
"and they also which pierced him,'
shall see him when he comes.

IT WILL BE UNEXPECTED BY THE GREAT MAJORITY

"Behold, I come as a thief. Blessed
is he that watcheth" (Rev. 16: 15). "If
therefore thou shalt not watch, I will
come on thee as a thief" (Rev. 3: 3).
"But the day of the Lord will come as
a thief in the night" (2 Pet. 3: 10). "For
yourselves know perfectly that the day
of the Lord so cometh as a thief in the
night." "For when they shall say,
Peace and safety, then sudden destruction cometh upon them . . . and they
shall not escape" (1 Thess. 5: 2, 3).
"And take heed to yourselves, lest at
any time your hearts be overcharged
with surfeiting, and drunkenness, and
cares of this life, and so that day come
upon you unawares. For as a snare

world before the flood. The millions of earth will be sleeping in carnal security, thousands dreaming of millennial glory. Oh, the surprize and disappointment of the masses in that great day! Never since the foundation of the world has there been a day like this, in the surprize and terror with which it will break upon the thoughtless millions of the population. Business and pleasure will occupy the minds of men, as usual, up to the close of the preceding day. The sun will rise and set with the same placid majesty, and as he sinks beneath the western horizon, he will fling his smiling radiance, in the same bountiful profusion, upon an admiring world. Myriads will go to rest dreaming of future years of wealth and happiness; but the loud blast of the "trump of God" will awake them to sleep no more, and looking up, they will see the heavens on fire.

The worldling, elated with schemes

of opulence and splendor, will suddenly
find his visions dispelled by the light of
eternity and the despairing cry, "The
Judge is come!" The astounded sen-
ate will suddenly break up at the crash
of the conflicting elements and, hurry-
ing away in wild confusion, see that the
great Legislator is come. The ermined
judge and the manacled prisoner will
hear themselves alike summoned without ceremony to the great tribunal. The
miser, counting his gold or reckoning
his profits, will be panic-stricken by the
knell that tells him gold has no more
value, and that his priceless soul is forever lost, in seeking a burst bubble.
The procrastinating trifler, dreaming of
mercy after years of worldly pleasure,
will be filled with dismay to see that
the day of grace is past and the hour
of retribution come. The anxious spec-
ulator, the busy merchant, the thriving
tradesman, racking imagination with
schemes of gain, panting to reach the

goal of wealth and revel in earthly aggrandizement, without one thought of God or eternity intruding on the vision of anticipated bliss, will be struck with terror to find the delusive mirage break up before the flare of the flaming skies and the catastrophe of a ruined world. The atheist, who denied God's being, will be appalled at the sight of his person. The Demases, who have forsaken him for the world; the Judases, who have betrayed him for silver; and all the host of apostates and blasphemers who have despised his name and trampled on his blood—these will stand aghast when the great day of his wrath shall break upon their sight.

It was an awful night in Egypt when every family rose up to bewail its firstborn struck with death; it was a day of terrible vengeance when the siege of Jerusalem closed with the crash of a ruined city over 1,100,000 dead bodies; it was a day of anger when the deluge burst upon a degenerate world and overwhelmed its despairing millions in one common grave—but this day exceeds them all: for it is the day when time shall have run its course, when universal retribution shall be awarded, when God himself shall come down to take vengeance on them that know him not, and when pent-up fires shall envelop the earth in a general conflagration. Throughout the New Testament the most solemn charges and warnings are given to the church to be ready for that great and awful event. "Watch therefore; for ye know not what hour your Lord doth come" (Matt. 24: 42). "Therefore be ye also ready: for in such an hour as ye think not the Son of man cometh" (v. 44). While to the masses Christ's coming will be a great surprize, his faithful church will be "looking for and hasting unto the coming of the day of God." "But ye, brethren, are not in darkness, that that day should overtake you as a thief. Ye are all the children of light, and the children of the day: we are not of the night, nor of darkness. Therefore let us not sleep, as do others; but let us watch and be sober" (1 Thess. 5: 4-6).

Saints and Angels Will Accompany Him

"Them also which sleep in Jesus will God bring with him" (1 Thess. 4: 14). "At the coming of our Lord Jesus Christ with all his saints" (1 Thess. 3: 13). "Behold, the Lord cometh with ten thousand of his saints, to execute judgment upon all" (Jude 14: 15). These texts have been used by millennium teachers to prove that Christ will come first **for** his saints, and afterwards **with** his saints. Thus, they attempt to show that there will be two comings of Christ future. But a careful study of the sub-

ject reveals the fact that when Christ
comes for his saints, or the church, he
will receive them into the eternal heav-
en of heavens, and thus give them their
eternal reward in resurrected and glorified bodies. When he descends from
heaven, he will bring with him the spirits of them which "sleep in Jesus"—the
souls that have been resting in paradise.
They will reanimate the bodies just
raised from the dead, after which they
will be caught up "to meet the Lord in
the air" and be forever with him. Thus,
in the same advent Christ will be ac-
companied by the saints and also receive them unto eternal rewards. The
angels will also accompany him. "For
the Son of man shall come in the glory
of his Father with his angels; and then
he shall reward every man according to
his works" (Matt. 16: 27). "When the
Son of man shall come in his glory, and
all the holy angels with him" (Matt.
25: 31). "When the Lord Jesus shall

be revealed from heaven with his mighty angels" (2 Thess. 1: 7).

He Will Appear Suddenly

"But of the times and seasons, brethren, ye have no need that I write unto you. For yourselves know perfectly that the day of the Lord so cometh as a thief in the night. For when they shall say, Peace and safety; then sudden destruction cometh upon them" (1 Thess. 5: 1-3). The affairs of the world will occupy the minds of men right up to the hour of judgment. As it was in the days of Noe, and also in the days of Lot, Jesus informs us, "thus shall it be in the day when the Son of man is revealed." The flood burst in upon the antediluvian world suddenly, like a mighty avalanche. In like manner came the destruction of Sodom and Gomorrah. In the day Lot went out of Sodom, God rained fire and brimstone from heaven and destroyed both Sodom and Gomorrah. Divine retribution was swiftly meted out to those ungodly cities. Just so will it be in the last day. "For as the lightning cometh out of the east, and shineth even unto the west; so shall also the coming of the Son of man be" (Matt. 24: 27). Suddenly as the flashing of lightning will the Lord Jesus "be revealed from heaven with his mighty angels, in flaming fire" (2 Thess. 1: 7, 8). "Watch ye therefore; . . . lest coming suddenly he find you sleeping" (Mark 13: 35, 36). "Surely I come quickly. Amen. Even so, come, Lord Jesus" (Rev. 22: 20).

WHO WILL BE READY?

The solemn charge Christ gave to the church in the present dispensation is to be ready. "Therefore be ye also ready: for in such an hour as ye think not the Son of man cometh" (Matt. 24:

44). The condition we must be in in order to be ready is expressed by John in these words: "Herein is our love made perfect, that we may have boldness in the day of judgment: because as he is, so are we in this world" (1 John 4: 17). We must be like Christ in moral purity—"perfect even as your Father . . . is perfect" (Matt. 5: 48); "righteous, even as he is" (1 John 3: 7); and pure, "even as he is pure" (1 John 3: 3). We must live upon the plane of his nature and possess his holiness. "Seeing then that all these things shall be dissolved, what manner of persons ought ye to be in all holy conversation and godliness." "Wherefore, beloved, seeing that ye look for such things, be diligent that ye may be found of him in peace, without spot, and blameless" (2 Pet. 3: 11, 14). These texts are very clear and to the point. When the great day of His wrath is come, only those will be able to stand

who in life were converted—born of the
Spirit of God—and as a result lived
righteously and holily. No man with
the least spot of sin will be able to stand
in the presence of the majesty and
awful glory of God, for the glory of his
presence will drive every unholy person
into everlasting destruction.

The Time Is Already Set

Some people talk of delaying the
Lord's coming, and then again, of hastening his coming. This betrays a lack
of understanding concerning God's
plan. No doubt from the very beginning God has meted out this world's
career and determined the time of its
end. Yes, the time is already set. "He
hath appointed a day, in the which he
will judge the world" (Acts 17: 31).
To "appoint" means to "determine,"
"fix," "settle." While Jesus was here

on earth he plainly said that the day and hour of judgment was already known to the Father. "But of that day and hour knoweth no man, no, not the angels of heaven, but my Father only" (Matt. 24: 36).

BUT NO MAN KNOWS THE EXACT DAY NOR HOUR

At different times men have arisen claiming to know the exact time of the Lord's return. William Miller, the founder of Adventism, set the time, and his followers in some places robed themselves and anxiously awaited the Lord's coming; but they were disappointed. I have in my possession positive proof that these same people at different times since have set a date for the Lord to come, but each time they were mistaken. In the face of such a plain declaration as the last text quoted, what utter folly it is for men to profess to know the exact date of the last day!

How clear are Christ's own words, "But of that day and hour **knoweth no man.**" However, Jesus gave a number of signs, saying, "When ye shall see these things come to pass, know that it is nigh, even at the door" (Mark 13: 29).

The Signs of His Coming

"The Pharisees also with the Sadducees came, and tempting desired him that he would show them a sign from heaven. He answered and said unto them, When it is evening, ye say, It will be fair weather; for the sky is red. And in the morning, It will be foul weather today; for the sky is red and lowering. O ye hypocrites, ye can discern the face of the sky; but can ye not discern the signs of the times?" (Matt. 16: 1-3).

There were many clear predictions in prophecy that related to the coming of the Messiah. Jacob upon his death-bed uttered the following: "The scepter shall not depart from Judah, nor a lawgiver from between his feet, until Shiloh come; and unto him shall the gathering of the people be" (Gen. 49: 10). The coming of Shiloh refers to the coming of Christ, the rest-giver. In this prophecy is predicted a continuous line of rulers in the seed of Judah, which was fulfilled from David to Christ. This prophecy was given to the chosen nation as a sign that when they should see a foreign ruler seize the scepter, they should know assuredly that the time had arrived for the Messiah to make his appearance. History proves that Herod was the first foreign prince that swayed the scepter in Judah, and it was in his reign that our Savior was born. Daniel was shown the very year that the Messiah would enter upon his earthly ministry (Dan. 9: 25). The prophet Micah gave the name of the very place of Christ's birth (Micah 5: 2; Matt. 2:

3-6). The prophet Isaiah foretold that
he should be born of a virgin (Isa. 7:
14). Malachi described his forerunner,
John. Isaiah also foretold the things
that should accompany his ministry
(Isa. 35:4-6). Zechariah told of the
exact manner of his entry into Jerusalem.

Many more prophecies could be given
that clearly related to the Messiah's
coming, and all of which were fulfilled
to the letter when he came. If the
Pharisees and Sadducees, with the Jewish nation in general, had been spiritual,
they would have understood these
things and accepted Christ. But being
spiritually blind, they placed wrong
constructions upon the predictions of
Christ's coming, and as a result, he did
not meet their anticipations; hence they
rejected and stumbled at him. They
expected that he would come with pomp
and great display, set up an earthly
kingdom, and make them a flourishing

empire in the earth. But instead, he came in a humble manner, preached to the poor, associated with the despised and rejected, and taught that his kingdom was not of this world.

Thus blinded to the true mission of Christ, the Jews understood not that he was the Messiah promised. There were, however, a few spiritual-minded men in Israel who understood the predictions of prophecy, and accepted him to the salvation of their souls. The Pharisees and Sadducees desired a special sign from heaven to prove that he was the Messiah. These "whited sepulchers,". although versed in worldly wisdom, and well read in the books of prophecy, able also to discern the face of the sky, were spiritually blinded and could not discern the signs of the times.

Beloved reader, the same is true of the masses today. The words of Jesus spoken to the Pharisees are very applicable at the present time—"O ye

hypocrites, ye can discern the face of
the sky; but can ye not discern the signs
of the times?"   The wisdom of this
world is searching out the deep things
of science, botany, astronomy, etc.
Great and mighty inventions are being
studied out; and, in fact, on almost all
lines the world is being enlightened,
and knowledge is increasing. But in
respect to spiritual things and the signs
of the times, the world in general is
ignorant and blind.

In Matt. 24: 3 the disciples asked Jesus, "What shall be the sign of thy
coming and of the end of the world?"
In the remainder of the chapter, he pro-
ceeded to show them things that would
take place prior to and during the awful
destruction of Jerusalem, and the ca-
lamities that would befall the Jewish
nation. He also gave them a number
of signs by which they might know that
when "these things come to pass," his

coming was near, "even at the door."
We will first consider—

SIGNS IN THE WORLD IN GENERAL

By referring to Dan. 12: 4, we learn
that in the "time of the end, many shall
run to and fro, and knowledge shall be
increased." It is no doubt true that this
text has reference to the entire Christian dispensation; but the great burden
of it we now see fulfilled in the closing
days of the current era. In olden times
the best means of conveyance were the
camel and the donkey on land, and the
sailboat on water. Since most of the
traveling was done on foot, it was very
slow and tedious. A very limited part
of the earth's area was known to the
civilized world. The largest body of
water generally known was the Med-
iterranean Sea, also called the "Great
Sea." But in our day, how changed are
conditions! Practically every nook and
corner of the globe has been penetrated

by enlightened and civilized mankind.
The great oceans have been circumnav-
igated, and mighty steamships plow the
seas. We have railroads, electric lines,
automobiles, and flying-machines all in
use; and almost with lightning rapidity
the multitudes of earth are running to
and fro. The increase of knowledge is
seen everywhere. The great inventions
of modern times, such as wireless tele-
graphy and many other things, which
are a public demonstration of this fact,
are the marvel of this age. By the use
of modern invention man is able to number the stars, and tell us the names
thereof. He measures their distance
from the earth, and reveals to us the
mysteries of the galaxies on high; he
delves into the strata of the rock, and
in the stone book of nature reads to us
the history of the ages.

Modern discoveries also contribute
to the increase of knowledge among the
people of earth.

Nations that have been uncultured and uncivilized for ages are today opening their doors to modern education, civilization, and enlightenment. The dark superstitions that have held these millions fast for long centuries, are giving way to the light of truth.

But right in the face of this enlightenment of the peoples of earth, is the fact that wickedness is continuing prevalent everywhere. Many of our pulpit orators are telling the people that the world is growing better. Some of them are looking for a glorious reign of universal righteousness, peace, and blessedness just prior to the Lord's coming. They refer to what science and education have done, and point to the accessions to the nominal church as proof. Because sin in our day is not assuming the barbarous forms which characterized the Dark Ages or heathen nations, some people are led to believe that a state of righteousness is rapidly spreading over the world, and that soon a triumphant reign of peace will be realized throughout the length and breadth of the earth—a time when righteousness shall cover the earth as the waters cover the sea. Under such a false hope and belief, millions of people are being lulled to sleep in carnal security while standing on the very brink of destruction and ruin, while the awful judgments of God are hanging over this doomed world, ready to burst in upon its sleeping myriads. Oh, may God in pity awaken man to discern the signs of the times! At the very time these "peace and safety" advocates are soothing the people with such false ideas, "then sudden destruction cometh upon them, as travail upon a woman with child; and they shall not escape" (1 Thess. 5: 3).

The entire tenor of the apostle's teaching in 1 Thess. 5: 1-8 shows that the moral state of the world in general will be one of spiritual lethargy, of slumber and indifference, right up to the moment of final judgment. This harmonizes with the statement of Christ as recorded in Luke 21: 34, 35: "And take heed to yourselves, lest at any time your hearts be overcharged with surfeiting, and drunkenness, and cares of this life, and so that day come upon you unawares. For as a snare shall it come on all them that dwell on the face of the whole earth." While this is a solemn charge to the church, it nevertheless reveals the condition of things generally, right up to the hour of judgment. Look at the masses today. Are they not given to surfeiting? This means excessive eating and drinking, a general time of festivity and revelling. Are not people today making a god of their belly? The hearts of the people are waxed so gross with these things that it is really hard to attract their attention long enough to listen to the gospel.

And drunkenness—look at the figures!
National prohibition is not a reality yet.
Four billion five hundred million gallons of beer alone are said to be consumed yearly.   This, as one writer
states, would make a row of beer-bar-
rels touching each other, fifty thousand
miles long, or twice around the world.
America's annual drink bill is said to
be over $2,000,000,000.   An estimate
based on the report of the Commissioner
of Internal Revenue, for the year ending June 30, 1915, makes America's
retail drink bill for that year about $2,-
552,385,897.25.   In 1913, 143,300,000
gallons of whisky were consumed, and
this with 18,000 fewer saloons; an increase of 7,500,000 gallons over the
previous year. Think of it! Look at
the mighty stream of damnation and
misery and crime that follows this
cursed traffic. This old world is now
tottering under a heavy weight of crime
and misery and sin that is being prac-

tised on every hand. In 1913 no less than 7,707,000,000 cigars and 14,012,-000,000 cigarets were smoked. Patrons of the pipe smoked 403,200,000 pounds of tobacco, or 9,400,000 pounds more than in 1912. Users of snuff disposed of 32,200,000 pounds of tobacco. I give these figures simply to show where the people's money goes. It is spent to satisfy a corrupt and sinful appetite.

While it is true that the Bible teaches a general spread of the gospel over all the earth, and the glorious triumph of Christ's kingdom and church in the evening of this dispensation, yet it also teaches that "the wicked shall do wickedly; and none of the wicked shall understand." As we look around in the light of truth, we see that wickedness is abounding on every hand. Sin is not confined to heathen nations alone; for in this enlightened America and in so-called Christian Europe, which embrace much of the light, knowledge, and im-

provement of the age, and which send
the missionary force of the world,
wickedness and deception abound.
Take up the daily newspaper and scan
its pages, and you will there see a rec-
ord of facts that verifies the truth of this
statement: brutal murders, highway
robberies, suicides, strikes, lynchings,
and appalling wars, that make us shud-
der at the scene. The printing-press,
which is so useful for the glorious
spread of the gospel to the ends of the
earth, and whose numberless sheets
might be like 'leaves of the tree of life
for the healing of the nations,' is used
by false teachers to propagate soul-
destroying doctrines of devils. The
worst of deception is being practised
upon the people everywhere.

The prophet Joel evidently speaks of
the time just prior to the end, when he
says: "Put ye in the sickle; for the harvest is ripe; come, get ye down; for
the press is full, the fats overflow; for

their wickedness is great" (Joel 3:13). Light rates the sinfulness of sin, and as the light is rapidly increasing in all the earth, sin is becoming exceeding sinful.

Surely the foregoing is sufficient to convince reasonable minds that wickedness will be prevalent in the earth right up to the coming of the Lord, and that no millennium of universal righteousness will take place before he comes. We will next consider

THE SIGNS OF THE TIMES AMONG PROFESSED CHRISTIANS

The general spirit of revelry and festivity so prevalent today is by no means confined to the non-professing classes. The multitudes of professing Christians are in these things marching hand in hand with the world. Festivals, fishing-pond and cake-walk lotteries, kissing-bees, and such like performances are in many places taking the place of the Holy Ghost prayer- and testimony-

meetings of former years. Allow me to
insert the following from the late Bishop
R. S. Foster, of the Methodist Episco-
pal Church. It well illustrates the moral
condition of the great masses of professed Christianity today.

"The ball, the theater, nude and lewd
art, social luxuries, with all their loose
moralities, are making inroads into the
sacred enclosure of the church; and as
a satisfaction for all this worldliness,
Christians are making a great deal of
Lent and Easter and Good Friday, and
church ornamentations. It is the old
trick of Satan. The Jewish church
struck on that rock, the Romish church
was wrecked on the same, and the
Protestant church is fast reaching the
same doom.

"Our great dangers, as we see them,
are assimilation to the world, neglect
of the poor, substitution of the form for
the fact of godliness, abandonment of
discipline, a hireling ministry, an im-

pure gospel, which, summed up, is a fashionable church. That Methodists should be liable to such an outcome, and that there should be signs of it in a hundred years from the 'sail-loft,' seems almost the miracle of history; but who that looks about him today can fail to see the fact?

"Do not Methodists, in violation of God's Word and their own discipline, dress as extravagantly and as fashionably as any other class? Do not the ladies, and often the wives and daughters of the ministry, put on 'gold and pearls and costly array'? Would not the plain dress insisted upon by John Wesley, Bishop Asbury, and worn by Hester Ann Rogers, Lady Huntingdon, and many others equally distinguished, be now regarded in Methodist circles as fanaticism? Can any one going into the Methodist church in any of our chief cities distinguish the attire of the communicants from that of the theater and

ball goers? Is not worldliness seen in
the music? Elaborately dressed and
ornamented choirs, who in many cases
make no profession of religion and are
often sneering skeptics, go through a
cold artistic or operatic performance,
which is as much in harmony with spiritual worship as an opera or theater.
Under such worldly performance spirituality is frozen to death.

"Formerly every Methodist attended
class and gave testimony of experiment-
al religion. Now the class-meeting is
attended by very few, and in many
churches abandoned. Seldom the
stewards, trustees, and leaders of the
church attend class. Formerly nearly
every Methodist prayed, testified, or exhorted in prayer-meeting. Now but
very few are heard. Formerly shouts
and praises were heard; now such dem-
onstrations of holy enthusiasm and joy
are regarded as fanaticism.

"Worldly socials, fairs, festivals, concerts, and such like have taken the place of the religious gatherings, revival meetings, class- and prayer-meetings of earlier days.

"How true that the Methodist discipline is a dead letter! Its rules forbid the wearing of gold or pearls or costly array; yet no one ever thinks of disciplining its members for violating them. They forbid the reading of such books and the taking of such diversions as do not minister to godliness; yet the church itself goes to shows and frolics and festivals and fairs, which destroy the spiritual life of the young as well as the old. The extent to which this is now carried on is appalling. The spiritual death it carries in its train will only be known when the millions it has swept into hell stand before the judgment.

"The early Methodist ministers went forth to sacrifice and to suffer for Christ. They sought not places of ease

and affluence, but of privation and suffering. They gloried not in their big
salaries, fine parsonages, and refined
congregations, but in the souls that had
been won for Jesus. Oh, how changed!
A hireling ministry will be a feeble, a
timid, a truckling, a time-serving ministry, without faith, endurance, and holy
power. Methodism formerly dealt in
the great central truth. Now the pulpits deal largely in generalities and in
popular lectures. The glorious doctrine
of entire sanctification is rarely heard
and seldom witnessed in the pulpits."

In the foregoing thoughts as expressed by Bishop Foster, we can truly
see the sad condition of Methodism and,
I may add, of Protestantism as a whole.
In the light of these facts, how dare men
say that the world is growing better?
"And because iniquity shall abound, the
love of many shall wax cold" (Matt.
24: 12). Though this text no doubt has
reference to the great apostasy of the

past, yet how awfully true is its fulfilment today! Many who were once
powers in the hands of God are today
lifeless. Beloved reader, how is it with
you? Is that your condition? Was
there a time in your life when you enjoyed more of the love of God than you
do now? a time when you loved secret
prayer, when you were more devoted?
O dear ones, let us not sleep as do others,
but let us watch and be sober! The
warm, fiery testimonies and prayers
once given and offered by many are
changed today to dry, cold, and lifeless
ones. The multitudes of professed
Christians today are "lovers of pleasure
more than lovers of God; having a form
of godliness, but denying the power
thereof." You can get more church-
members to take an active part in a
social or festival than in a good old-
fashioned prayer- and testimony-meet-
ing, and they will enjoy it better.

In fact, the sectarian world, as a

whole, has but a form of godliness; a
mere outward form, without life and
power in the soul—the hull without the
kernel. The old-time fire, shouts of joy,
and spiritual meetings of former days
are replaced by cold, dead worship.
This is the fallen condition of sect
Babylon everywhere. Clear, radical
conversions are seldom witnessed in
their meetings. The sermons are dry
and stale. The ministers, instead of going forth under a divine call and commission, baptized with the Holy Ghost
and fire, enter the work as a profession,
the same as a doctor or a lawyer takes
up his work—simply for the money that
is in it. They care not for the souls of
men, but seek the applause and fat
pocketbooks of their members. Well
hath the prophet said, "Ye eat the fat,
and ye clothe you with the wool, . . .
but ye feed not the flock" (Ezek. 34: 3).
These "blind," sleepy, "greedy" watch-
men "can never have enough," but

"they all look to their own way, every one for his gain, from his quarter" (Isa. 56:11). They teach for hire, and divine for money: "yet will they lean upon the Lord, and say, Is not the Lord among us?" (Micah 3:11). They teach "smooth things and prophesy deceit" (Isa. 30:10). They tell the people that they can not live free from sin; that sanctification is not attainable in this life, etc. Thus the hearts of the people are turned away "from the truth," and turned unto "fables" (2 Tim. 4:1-4). These false doctrines are so instilled into them that when the sound doctrine of truth is presented, they will not endure it. Who dare deny that these are present facts?

"This know also, that in the last days perilous times shall come. For men shall be lovers of their own selves, covetous, boasters, proud, blasphemers, disobedient to parents, unthankful, unholy, without natural affection, truce-

breakers, false accusers, incontinent,
fierce, despisers of those that are good,
traitors, heady, high-minded, lovers of
pleasure more than lovers of God; having a form of godliness, but denying the
power thereof: from such turn away"
(2 Tim. 3: 1-5). What a picture of the
present state of things! No doubt such
characters as these lived in Paul's day.
But the peril that he predicts is that
these characters were to have a "form
of godliness." Such has been the case
ever since the rise of sectarianism. "But
evil men and seducers shall wax worse
and worse, deceiving, and being deceived" (2 Tim. 3: 13). The prophet
Daniel, in describing the latter-day
glory of the church, says, "Many shall
be purified, and made white, and tried."
But the prophet would have us to know
that at the very same time "the wicked
shall do wickedly: and none of the
wicked shall understand; but the wise
shall understand" (Dan. 12: 10).

Another proof that the world in general will not be in a state of righteousness when Christ comes, is the fact that the Scriptures so frequently state that his coming will be unexpected as a thief in the night. "For when they shall say, Peace and safety, then sudden destruction cometh upon them, as travail upon a woman with child; and they shall not escape" (1 Thess. 5:3). "And as it was in the days of Noah, so shall it be in the days of the Son of man. They did eat, they drank, they married wives, they were given in marriage, until the day Noah entered into the ark, and the flood came, and destroyed them all. Likewise also as it was in the days of Lot; they did eat, they drank, they bought, they sold, they planted, they builded; but the same day that Lot went out of Sodom it rained fire and brimstone from heaven, and destroyed them all. Even thus shall it be in the day when the Son of man is revealed"

(Luke 17: 26-30). This text clearly proves that as destruction was to the antediluvian world and the cities of Sodom and Gomorrah unexpected, so will it be when the Son of man is revealed. If the world were in a general state of righteousness up to the coming of the Lord, it would not be unexpected as a thief in the night; for the truly ready are "looking for and hasting unto the coming of the day of God." "Ye, brethren, are not in darkness, that that day should overtake you as a thief. Ye are all the children of light, and the children of the day: we are not of the night, nor of darkness. Therefore, let us not sleep, as do others; but let us watch and be sober." From this scripture we learn that to the righteous, Christ's coming will not be as a thief, while to the masses of the world his coming will be as a thief.

While the Word of God does not teach that this world will be in the same state of wickedness that Sodom was, prior to the end, yet we are forced to the conclusion that it is in the state to-day that Sodom was. It might be well to take a brief look at the sins of Sodom as recorded in Ezek. 16: 49, 50—"Behold, this was the iniquity of thy sister Sodom: pride, fulness of bread, and abundance of idleness was in her and in her daughters, neither did she strengthen the hand of the poor and needy. And they were haughty, and committed abomination before me: therefore, I took them away as I saw good." The sins of Sodom are the sins of today; and as the people of today have greater light than had the people of Sodom, their wickedness is far more sinful. Jesus says: "It shall be more tolerable for Sodom in that day than for you."

The first sin of Sodom placed on the list is pride. In the fear of God we declare that it is the greatest evil of today.

Pride is sending more souls to hell than liquor. Because of pride, spirituality is frozen to death. Where will you go to see the latest styles and fashions; the largest display of jewelry? Enter a large meeting-house in our towns and cities and look upon the persons of those around that which is called the Lord's table, and you will find the answer. The slaves who are ruled by the goddess of Fashion can be numbered by the millions in the Christian sects. The sectarian world is flooded with a proud hireling ministry who dare not cry out against this prevalent evil. "Love not the world, neither the things that are in the world. If any man love the world, the love of the Father is not in him. For all that is in the world, the lust of the flesh, and the lust of the eyes, and the pride of life, is not of the Father but is of the world" (1 John 2: 15, 16). Some cry that we had better be out of the world than out of fashion. This is

true, but if people obtain salvation they
will be saved out of the world. "If ye
were of the world, the world would love
his own: but because ye are not of the
world, but I have chosen you out of the
world, therefore the world hateth you"
(John 15: 19). Amen. Those who possess pure and undefiled religion keep
themselves unspotted from the world
(Jas. 1: 27).

Next among the sins of Sodom was
"fulness of bread"—neither did they
strengthen the hand of the poor and
needy. "An abundance of idleness was
in her." This is also one of the great
evils of today. The present trend of affairs is to grind down the poor and lift
up the rich. While wealth and plenty
abound, thousands of homeless men,
women, and children, in our cities are
starving for bread. As we look around
we see the laboring classes dissatisfied.
There is a lack of confidence in the
heads of our government, and a lack

of confidence in each other. Strikes by
the score, followed by riots and blood-
shed, are yearly occurrences. Two
mighty forces are today gathering in
bitter opposition. The money-masters
on the one side, and the dissatisfied
hosts of laborers on the other.

This line of truth could be very much
drawn out, but we deem the foregoing
sufficient to show what the general condition of the professed Christian world
is to be just prior to the second advent.
And I believe that present facts bear
us out in stating that we are living in
the very times portrayed in these scriptures.

SIGNS OF THE TIMES IN THE CHURCH

The Scriptures clearly teach that out
of the maze of confusion and dead
formality, before described, the Lord
would gather to himself a pure church,
separated from sin and the world, and
that this church would help to consti-

tute his pure and holy bride, made ready
for his coming. Just such a work is now
being accomplished. His bride is now
being made ready. "And to her was
granted that she should be arrayed in
fine linen, clean and white: for the fine
linen is the righteousness of the saints."

The gathering together of God's people out of all the sects into which they
had been scattered in the cloudy and
dark day, was to be accomplished before the end. This gathering of the
elect is now taking place. The Scriptures also teach that before the end
there will be a restoration of the whole
truth and that the light of the pure gospel will shine forth as in primitive
times: "At evening time it shall be
light." Reader, we are living in that
very time, hence we rightly conclude
that now is the **evening** time of the
Christian dispensation. With the restoration of the pure church, and the
sounding forth of the whole gospel, the

gifts of the Spirit are being demon-
strated as in primitive times. The sick
are being healed, miracles wrought in
the name of Jesus, devils cast out; and,
in fact, nearly all the mighty demon-
strations of God's miraculous power
manifested in the midst of his people
in primitive times are being repeated today. And best of all, in this time of the
end many are being "purified, and made
white, and tried." Jesus gave the
preaching of the gospel of the kingdom
in all the world (see Matt. 24: 14) as
a positive sign of his near coming. In
fulfilment of this scripture, a missionary
spirit is today inspiring the church of
Christ and a host of self-sacrificing ministers are going forth having the "everlasting gospel to preach unto them that
dwell on the earth, and to every nation,
and kindred, and tongue, and people."
Millions of copies of the Bible are being
distributed among all nations in their
different languages. And by the aid

of the modern printing-press, many tons of pure gospel literature in the form of papers, tracts, and books, are being sent yearly to every part of the earth. By our modern, swift means of transit, this great work of evangelizing the world is hastened. Many other signs in the church could be given, such as its conflicts with the false religions of earth; but these points are fully covered in my book Christ's Kingdom and Reign.

A Description of His Coming

"But in those days, after that tribulation, the sun shall be darkened, and the moon shall not give her light, and the stars of heaven shall fall, and the powers that are in heaven shall be shaken. And then shall they see the Son of man coming in the clouds, with great power and glory. And then shall he send his

angels, and shall gather together his
elect from the four winds, from the uttermost part of the earth, to the uttermost part of heaven" (Mark 13: 24-27).
The same description is given by Matthew, except that he adds, "And then
shall all the tribes of the earth mourn."

"And there shall be signs in the sun,
and in the moon, and in the stars; and
upon the earth distress of nations, with
perplexity; the sea and the waves roaring; men's hearts failing them for fear,
and for looking after those things
which are coming on the earth: for the
powers of heaven shall be shaken. And
then shall they see the Son of man coming in a cloud, with power and great
glory. And when these things begin to
come to pass, then look up, and lift up
your heads; for your redemption draweth nigh" (Luke 21: 25-28). This is a
description of Christ's coming as given
by Christ himself. In Rev. 6: 12-17, we
have an allusion to the same great event

in very similar language. "And I beheld when he had opened the sixth seal, and, lo, there was a great earthquake; and the sun became black as sackcloth of hair, and the moon became as blood; and the stars of heaven fell unto the earth, even as a fig-tree casteth her untimely figs, when she is shaken of a mighty wind. And the heavens departed as a scroll when it is rolled together; and every mountain and island were moved out of their places. And the kings of the earth, and the great men, and the rich men, and chief captains, and the mighty men, and every bondman, and every freeman, hid themselves in the dens and in the rocks of the mountains; and said to the mountains and rocks, Fall on us, and hide us from the face of him that sitteth on the throne, and from the wrath of the Lamb: for the great day of his wrath is come; and who shall be able to stand?"

The picture presented in the foregoing scriptures is almost beyond our comprehension. Such a day this world has never seen. No wonder it is elsewhere termed "that great day of God Almighty," "a day of wrath," "a day of vengeance," and "the great and the terrible day of the Lord." Taking all three accounts together, it appears that shortly before the revelation of Christ from heaven, the entire universe will begin to tremble. The sun shall be darkened, the moon shall no longer give her light, and the stars of heaven shall fall. This can all be visible to man, as one side of earth is day at the same time that the other side is night. The very powers that are in heaven shall be shaken, and the heavens themselves shall depart as a scroll when it is rolled together. Here Jesus was giving us a clear description of his coming, which event was to follow the tribulation which befell the Jewish nation in the destruction of their city.

According to Luke the signs in the sun, moon, and stars are spoken of in contradistinction to what would take place "upon the earth." This proves that the literal heavens are referred to. At this same time, when the powers of heaven are being shaken, upon the earth there will be distress of nations, with perplexity, the sea and the waves roaring. No doubt this is the same time of which Isaiah spoke when he said, "The earth is moved exceedingly. The earth shall reel to and fro like a drunkard" (Isa. 24: 19, 20). Amid such scenes as this, it is said, men's hearts shall fail them for fear, and all the tribes of the earth shall mourn. And then the kings of the earth, the great men, the rich men, and, in fact, the whole world, caught as in a "snare," shall run to and fro trying to hide in places of safety.

Matthew tells us all this, as described, is "the sign of the Son of man in heaven." To the church these words are given: "And when these things begin to come to pass, then look up, and lift up your heads; for your redemption draweth nigh" (Luke 21: 28). That is, do not be fearful; have "boldness," look up, for Christ is about to appear. "Then shall they see the Son of man coming in a cloud with power and great glory" (v. 27). "For the Lord himself shall descend from heaven with a shout, and with the voice of the archangel, and with the trump of God." "The Lord Jesus shall be revealed from heaven with his mighty angels, in flaming fire." O reader, are you ready to stand amid such scenes as herein described? It will mean something to have boldness in that awful day when we stand amid the crash of empires, the burning skies, the catastrophe of a ruined world, and the flaming fire of the "wrath of the Lamb."

The Object of His Coming

Concerning what will take place when Christ comes there is a great diversity of opinion and teaching. Some claim that the second advent of Christ will usher in a great day of salvation to the teeming millions who in life neglected the opportunities to be saved or who did not have the privileges of the gospel, and that at that time a literal kingdom of God will be established over all the earth. Others claim that when Christ comes, he will resurrect the righteous that are dead, and then establish his throne in the city of Jerusalem and reign for the conversion of the Jews. At the close of this supposed millennial reign, he will resurrect the wicked, who will then be judged and punished. The righteous, it is claimed, will not be judged, but will rather take part in judging the nations.

I shall not attempt to present all the

conflicting views of millennium teachers, for as one writer states it, "No two
of them fix it up the same way." The
theories are about as numerous as the
advocates, and these can be numbered
by the thousands. In not a single text
in the four Gospels is there a hint of a
millennial reign to follow the second
advent. Not once did Christ mention
the word "millennium." Nor can it be
found in any of the nineteen epistles
that help to constitute the New Testament. The book of Acts is also free
from its mention. I want to emphasize
this point. The word "millennium"
can not be found in the Bible. Why so
much talk of it in this day and age of
the world? "Millennium" is a Latin
term meaning a thousand years, and the
only mention of a thousand years in connection with any reign of Christ and his
people is in the book of symbols (Revelation 20). And there is no mention in
that scripture of Christ's reigning on

this earth, nor of the saints' reigning here after the resurrection. There is no mention of a thousand years intervening between the resurrection of the righteous and the wicked. "The rest of the dead" help to make up what is termed "the first resurrection." All these points are fully treated in Book I of this series.

In the face of all the confusing and contradictory pre-millennial doctrines, the plain testimony of Scripture stands out in clear teaching that the revelation of Jesus Christ from heaven will be the hour of the resurrection of the dead, the general judgment, the reward of the righteous in heaven, the punishment of the wicked in hell, and the burning up and passing away of the earth.

The Resurrection of the Dead

There will be millions of people, good and bad, living upon the earth when

Christ comes, who shall not see death;
but "shall all be changed, in a moment,
in the twinkling of an eye, at the last
trump: for the trumpet shall sound, and
the dead shall be raised incorruptible,
and we shall be changed" (1 Cor. 15:
51, 52). This text plainly teaches that
when the trumpet shall sound, the dead
will be raised and the living will be
changed. The question then is, When
will this trumpet sound? The answer is
given in 1 Thess. 4:16: "For the Lord
himself shall descend from heaven with
a shout, and with the voice of the archangel, and with the trump of God: and
the dead in Christ shall rise first." Language could not express more clearly
that the resurrection of the dead will
take place when Jesus comes. In John
6 Jesus repeated several times concerning the righteous, "I will raise him up
at the last day." Martha, in addressing
Jesus concerning her dead brother, Lazarus, said, "I know that he shall rise

again in the resurrection **at the last day**" (John 11:24). The doctrine of the resurrection of the dead is well founded in Holy Writ. It seems to have been the belief of the orthodox church in all ages. The patriarch Job testified on this point, "And though after my skin worms destroy this body, yet in my flesh shall I see God" (Job 19:26). Isaiah adds his testimony as a firm believer in a future resurrection: "Thy dead men shall live, together with my dead body shall they arise. Awake and sing, ye that dwell in the dust: for thy dew is as the dew of herbs, and the earth shall cast out her dead" (Isa. 26:19). This is spoken of in close connection with the following: "Behold, the Lord cometh out of his place to punish the inhabitants of the earth for their iniquity" (v. 21). The coming of the Lord will be the time of the resurrection. Daniel says, "And many of them that sleep in the dust of the earth shall awake, some

to everlasting life, and some to shame
and everlasting contempt" (Dan. 12:2).

When we come to the New Testament, we find Jesus boldly teaching the
resurrection to the Sadducees in the following language: "Ye do err, not knowing the Scriptures, nor the power of
God. For in the resurrection they
neither marry, nor are given in marriage, but are as the angels of God in
heaven. But as touching the resurrection of the dead, have ye not read that
which was spoken unto you by God,
saying, I am the God of Abraham, and
the God of Isaac, and the God of Jacob?
God is not the God of the dead, but of
the living. And when the multitude
heard this, they were astonished at his
doctrine" (Matt. 22: 29-33). This put
the Sadducees to silence (v. 34). Jesus
said to Martha, "I am the resurrection,
and the life: he that believeth in me,
though he were dead, yet shall he live"
(John 11: 25). Paul in his defense be-

fore Felix, in the presence of the high priest and elders of the Jews, boldly declared "that there shall be a resurrection of the dead, both of the just and unjust" (Acts 24: 15). Thus we could multiply texts of scripture to prove that there will be a resurrection of the dead, and that the same will take place on the last day of time, which will be the hour of Christ's second advent.

Christ's Resurrection an Assurance of Our Resurrection

That there will be a resurrection from the dead—a coming forth of real bodies that have for ages moldered back to mother dust—is denied by many of the schools of higher criticism today. It is astounding to find almost everywhere a large number of people who are becoming skeptical regarding the resurrection. Some teach that instead of the dead coming forth, the Lord will create new bodies the same as he created Adam in the beginning. In a sense this can be true, and yet not conflict with the fact of a real resurrection from the dead.

In the 15th chapter of First Corinthians we find an able defense of the resurrection of the dead by the apostle Paul. His argument is—"If the dead rise not, then is not Christ raised." There seems to have been some at Corinth, who admitted that Christ had risen again, but denied the resurrection of the dead. The Apostle's argument was that if Christ was raised from the dead, mankind may be raised: if mankind can not be raised from the dead, then the body of Christ was never raised. And since the whole structure of Christianity is built on the fact that Christ is risen and is at the right hand of God, ever living to make intercession for us, —to deny the resurrection is to strike at the very root of the Christian religion.

If it be true that Christ was not raised, then we have no hope and are yet in our sins. But Paul's argument reaches its climax in the bold declaration: **"But now is Christ risen from the dead,** and become the first-fruits of them that slept. For since by man [Adam] came death, by man [Christ Jesus] came also the resurrection of the dead. For as in Adam all die, even so in Christ shall all be made alive" (vs. 20-22).

The future resurrection of the dead hinges entirely on the fact that Christ is risen. And of his resurrection there is abundant proof. The evangelist, Matthew, who was an apostle of the Lord, records the fact that "the angel of the Lord descended from heaven, and came and rolled back the stone from the door, and sat upon it. His countenance was like lightning, and his raiment white as snow. And for fear of him the keepers did shake, and became as dead men" (Matt. 28:2-4). One writer describes this scene thus: 'A profound, solemn stillness reigns all around, broken only by the tread of the guards as they pace backwards and forwards before the tomb of the crucified Prince of peace. The grave lies mute and closed before us; its seal remains unbroken. It would seem that the reign of the pretended new King of Zion was gone forever. But what now? On a sudden the earth begins to tremble; the rocks are rent asunder all around with fearful crash; superhuman forms, bright as lightning and in garments white as snow, glide down from the heights of heaven to the garden. They are holy angels. One of these gracious messengers approaches the tomb, touches the mass of rock which held it closed, and in a moment the seals are burst, the ponderous stone is rolled away, and from the open portal of the grave there steps forth, radiant with heavenly glory, him who was dead!—

and, behold, "is alive forever more." '

From this angel that rolled the stone from the tomb, we have positive testimony of Christ's resurrection. "And the angel answered and said unto the women, Fear not ye, for I know that ye seek Jesus, which was crucified. He is not here; for he is risen, as he said. Come, see the place where the Lord lay. And go quickly, and tell his disciples that he has risen from the dead."

On several occasions before his death, Christ assured his disciples that after his death he would rise again on the third day. We have the recorded testimony of four inspired evangelists— Matthew, Mark, Luke, and John—that His resurrection actually took place. Angels from heaven testified the same truth to the women who came early to the sepulcher. Soon after, "when Jesus was risen early the first day of the week, he appeared first to Mary Magdalene" (Mark 16:9). Paul informs us "that he arose again the third day according to the Scriptures; and that he was seen of Cephas, then of the twelve: after that he was seen of above five hundred brethren at once; of whom the greater part remain unto this present, but some are fallen asleep. After that, he was seen of James; then of all the apostles. And last of all he was seen of me also, as of one born out of due time." (1 Cor. 15:4-8). In Acts 1:2, 3, it is further stated that "unto the apostles" "he showed himself alive after his passion by many infallible proofs, being seen of them forty days, and speaking of the things pertaining to the kingdom of God."

Thus we have the testimony of a multitude of witnesses that Christ actually rose from the dead. Nothing stands more historically true than this. It is equally certain that they saw him, not as a common man, nor as a ghost, but as their risen Lord—the one only Son

of God.   Thus Revelation assures us
that there will be a resurrection of the
body.   This hope the Christian church
now possesses; for he has "begotten us
again unto a lively hope by the resurrection of Jesus Christ from the dead"
(1 Pet. 1: 3).

In Millennial Dawnism it is taught
that Christ's identical body which was
laid in the tomb of Joseph of Arima-
thea, was not the one that was raised;
but such teaching is utter folly in the
face of the plain statements of Scripture.   In Luke 24: 3 we learn that the
women entered into the sepulcher, "and
found not the body of the Lord Jesus."
The angel told them the reason.   "He
is not here, but is risen."

The resurrection of Jesus was the
central theme and message of the apostles, which utterly confounded the Jews.
On the day of Pentecost, Peter declared
to them that the very Christ they were
instrumental in putting to death "hath

God raised up, whereof we all are witnesses" (Acts 2: 32). "When they
heard this they were pricked in their
hearts, and said . . . Men and brethren, what shall we do?" Again, when
questioned concerning the healing of
the lame man at the gate Beautiful, the
apostles boldly testified that the miracle
was wrought in the name of Christ,
"through faith in his name," and that
this was the same Prince of life they
had killed, "whom God hath raised
from the dead; whereof we are witnesses" (Acts 3: 15, 16). The Sadducees, "being grieved that they taught
the people, and preached through Jesus
the resurrection from the dead," laid
hands on them and brought them before
the rulers. Again Peter boldly declared, "Be it known unto you all, and
to all the people of Israel, that by the
name of Jesus Christ of Nazareth, whom
ye crucified, whom God raised from the

dead, even by him doth this man stand before you whole" (Acts 4:10).

Generally, those who oppose the resurrection endeavor to show that such a thing is incredible and utterly impossible. They cite such instances as bodies cremated and the ashes scattered to the winds, evaporating into air, or falling to the earth and being assimilated into the vegetable kingdom; and such as have been drowned in the sea and eaten by the fish, or such as have been eaten by cannibals. They argue that a resurrection of the body in such cases is absurd. We answer them in the language Paul used in his defense before King Agrippa—"Why should it be thought a thing incredible with you, that God should raise the dead?" (Acts 26:8). We maintain that it is reasonable and possible.

In this light, let it be remembered that "the Spirit of him that raised up Jesus from the dead . . . shall also

quicken your mortal bodies by his Spirit" (Rom. 8: 11). Again, it is said, "He
which raised up the Lord Jesus, shall
raise up us also by Jesus." People seem
to forget the power of Omnipotence.
The same mighty power that raised up
Christ from the dead shall raise us up
also. He is the "first-fruits of them that
slept." On the omnipotence of God we
take our stand and defy every attack
against the doctrine of the resurrection.
We scorn all attempts to wrest from us
our hope, through a supposed impossibility of the resurrection, as puny strug-
gles against the omnipotence of God.
'Did he not first construct a human form
from the dust of the earth? Did he not
breathe into a mass of clay the breath
of life? And when he again speaks,
shall it not be done? Can he not again
bring bone to bone, sinew to its sinew,
flesh to its flesh? Fear not, Christian!
Thy dust may be scattered to the winds
of heaven—but thy God is there. It may

repose in the lowest abyss of the grave
—he is there. It may dwell in the uttermost parts of the sea and even from
there he shall bring thee forth, incorruptible and glorious, like unto that
body which now receives the homage of
the angels around the throne. Thou
shalt be raised at the last day. Let us
"comfort one another with these
words." '

Yes, this is our hope and comfort.
"We look for the Savior, the Lord Jesus
Christ; who shall change our vile body,
that it may be fashioned like unto his
glorious body, according to the working
whereby he is able even to subdue all
things unto himself" (Phil. 3: 20, 21).
Just as the first-fruits and the first ripe
sheaf were offered to the Lord, Christ's
resurrection is the pledge and promise
of a coming harvest.

'Henceforth the grave holds but a
lease on the saints: because He rose,
we shall rise also. Through Christ, the

first-born, I see the grave giving up its dead; from the depths of the sea, from lonely wilderness and crowded church-yards they come—like the dews of the grass, an innumerable multitude. Risen Lord, we rejoice in thy resurrection, and hail it as the harbinger of our own. The first to come forth, thou art the elder brother of a family whose countless numbers Abraham saw in the dust of the desert, whose holy beauty he saw shining as the stars of heaven.'

In the light of science there is no incomprehensible enigma presented in the doctrine of the resurrection. In fact, the resurrection does not necessarily require that the identical flesh that composed the body when laid away in the grave shall compose the body raised in incorruption. No fact is more familiar to the student of science than that our present bodies are subject to continual change. As our bodies grow, new matter is added to them, besides

the repairing of what is continually
spent. In the course of a few years that
change is entire. Of the particles which
composed the body in infancy, not one
remains in youth; of those which filled
out the frame in youth, not one remains
in middle age; and so on. It is claimed
that every seven years the body has
undergone a complete change. But
mark well the fact that, through this
ever-changing process, **identity is not
lost.** Something abides; and this is the
most essential thing of all. Call it what
you may—the vital principle, the law of
assimilation and arrangement, the or-
ganic force—it remains permanent, and
as the old materials are thrown off they
are replaced with new. Paul goes deep
into this thought by presenting a simili-
tude in 1 Cor. 15: 36-38. This something, like a germ in the seed, to which
it corresponds, may lie dormant for
ages, and in God's appointed time, under divinely arranged conditions, awake

anew. God's appointed time will be
the morning of the resurrection. The
voice of Christ on this morning will be
one of the appointed conditions of our
resurrection.

There is another well-known fact in
science; that nothing is lost throughout
the vast universe. Mark well this fact:
whether our bodies evaporate and help
to compose the air we breathe. or
whether they are reduced to liquid, or
whether they are assimilated in the vegetable kingdom, **they remain; there is
nothing lost.** It is claimed that the very
elements which compose our material
bodies are found in the ground under-
neath our feet, and in the air which we
breathe. The elements which now compose our bodies have been, by natural
means, collected from all parts of the
world. How foolish, then, to assert that
the God who controls all things, and
governs them by his own law, can not
by his omnipotent power collect them

again from the dust of the ground, from the atmosphere about us, or from the depths of the sea. "With God all things are possible." As truly as Jesus' body, which was laid in Joseph's tomb, came forth a glorified and immortal body—for he "dieth no more," and "death hath no more dominion over him,"—so shall we be raised, and our "body fashioned like unto his glorious body."

"So also is the resurrection of the dead. It is sown in corruption; it is raised in incorruption: it is sown in dishonor; it is raised in glory: it is sown in weakness; it is raised in power: it is sown a natural body; it is raised a spiritual body" (1 Cor. 15: 42-44). Whatever difficulties may present themselves in connection with the resurrection, whatever obstacles of a miraculous or supernatural nature may to our minds appear—for in these things we are but limited in understanding—are easily

met by remembering the truth enun-
ciated by Christ himself in connection
with this very subject when he confounded those who did not believe in it;
namely, "Ye do err, not knowing the
Scriptures, nor the power of God."

The Body Will Be Resurrected

A number of millennium teachers
deny a resurrection of the body, but
claim that the soul will be resurrected
from the grave. This is virtually the
position taken in Millennium Dawn, by
C. T. Russell. He denies that Christ's
body, which was crucified on Calvary,
was ever raised from the tomb. There
are a few texts in the Old Testament
that speak of redeeming the soul from
the grave; but a careful examination
of these texts show that in the original
the regular word for grave—qeber—
is not found. But in these texts the He-

brew word translated "grave" is Sheol, which is equivalent to the Greek Hades. The grave (qeber) is the receptable of the body; while the unseen world (Sheol or Hades) is the receptacle of the soul between natural death and the resurrection. In this state the righteous are 'absent from the body, and present with the Lord,' and the wicked are "reserved unto the day of judgment to be punished"; "reserved in everlasting chains under darkness." These souls are conscious, and they continue to live while absent from their bodies. Peter plainly tells that while Christ's body was in the tomb his soul was in Hades (Acts 2: 25-32, A. S. V.). He and the converted thief were together in paradise.

At the time the angel descended and rolled away the stone, the Spirit of Christ reanimated the body, which came forth, for it was Christ's body that was crucified and laid in Joseph's tomb. The

angels said to the women, "Come, see
the place where the Lord lay." The
linen clothes were there, but the body
was gone. "He is not here: for he is
risen," was the glorious announcement.
In this same body he appeared on several occasions to his disciples. When
laid in the tomb, it was a natural body;
but when risen, it was a spiritual, incorruptible body. And just so it is stated
in Phil. 3: 21 that at the coming of the
Lord Jesus Christ "our vile body" will
be "fashioned like unto his glorious
body." Again, in 1 Cor. 15: 44, we read,
"It is sown a natural body; it is raised
a spiritual body." "This mortal [which,
of course, means this mortal body] shall
put on immortality" (1 Cor. 15: 53).
Here, then, we have sufficient proof that
the resurrection applies to the body and
not to the soul. At the time of the resurrection of Christ, it is said, "many
bodies of the saints which slept arose,
and came out of the graves."

NECESSITY OF RESURRECTION OF BODY

The deeds of life determine our future destiny. While the soul is the volitional part of our being—that which is held accountable to God—yet words are expressed through human tongues and lips, and deeds are performed by and through the members of the physical body. This is made clear in Rom. 6: 12, 13: "Let not sin therefore reign in your mortal body, that ye should obey it in the lusts thereof. Neither yield ye yourselves as instruments of unrighteousness unto sin: but yield yourselves unto God, as those that are alive from the dead, and your members as instruments of righteousness unto God." With the feet men dance, and with the feet they go to places of crime and wickedness. With the hands they steal, murder, etc. With the mouth they speak words of profanity and cursings against the holy and reverend name of Jehovah. And just as truly after we are saved,

do the members of our physical body
perform the functions of the purified
and redeemed soul that lives within.

Since the whole man—soul and body
—performs the acts which determine
his destiny, it is both reasonable and
necessary that with soul and body he
reap his reward.

The Bible plainly teaches three states
of the human spirit. (1) In union with
an animal body. This is our present
state, and terminates at death. (2) A
state in which the human spirit is separate from the animal body, and yet
has a conscious existence. This begins
with death and terminates with the resurrection from the dead. (3) The state
in which the spirit is reunited to the
body, raised immortal. This state begins at the resurrection and continues
forever.

The resurrection necessitates the survival of the soul after death. Jesus
made this clear in his teachings, which

confounded the Sadducees. They did not believe in the resurrection nor in the survival of the spirit after death. Jesus refuted their position by boldly quoting from Exodus the words of Jehovah, "I am the God of Abraham, and the God of Isaac, and the God of Jacob." Then he added, "God is not the God of the dead, but of the living" (Matt. 22: 32). Although the bodies of these three patriarchs had been slumbering in the tomb for ages, they themselves were still alive. God at that very time was their God; "not the God of the dead" — those moldered bodies — but "the God of the living"; that is, "the God of the **spirits** of all flesh." The very fact that the spirits of these men were living, conclusively proved that since death did not end all it was altogether possible and probable that their bodies would be raised. This argument confounded the Sadducee leaders. Paul informs us that "we must all appear be-

fore the judgment seat of Christ; that
every one may receive the things done
in his body, according to that he hath
done, whether it be good or bad" (2
Cor. 5: 10).

Man, as a whole, is both spirit and
body. This brings us to the considera-
tion of the third state of human spirits
—the condition in which the spirit will
be reunited with the body, raised immortal. Without the other, neither can
fulfil its destiny. This third state com-
mences with the resurrection at the last
day and continues forever. The body
is not only a habitation for the soul; it
is the soul's organ of communication, of
communion, and expression. The separation that we call death is a fruit and
penalty of sin. The ideal man—man as
he first existed in the thought of God
and as he will exist when fully restored
and glorified—will be an embodied
spirit. In glorified bodies will the
righteous reap their eternal reward

when death, the last enemy, is forever destroyed. "Both soul and body" of the wicked will be punished in hell.

Concerning the fact that man will rise with the same moral character with which he died, I quote from Thomas Chalmers: "The character wherewith we sink into the grave at death is the very character wherewith we shall reappear on the day of resurrection. The character which habit has fixed and strengthened through life, adheres, it would seem, to the disembodied spirit through the mysterious interval which separates the day of our dissolution from the day of our account—when it will again stand forth, the very image and substance of what it was, to the inspection of the Judge and the awards of the judgment-seat. The moral lineaments which be graven on the tablet of the inner man, and which every day of an unconverted life makes deeper and more indelible than before, will retain

the very impress they have gotten—un-
altered and uneffaced by the transition
from our present to our future state of
existence. There will be a dissolution,
and then a reconstruction of the body
from the sepulchral dust into which it
had moldered. But there will be
neither a dissolution nor a renovation
of the spirit, which, indestructible both
in character and essence, will weather
and retain its identity on the midway
passage between this world and the
next: so that at the time of quitting its
earthly tenement we may say, that if
unjust now, it will be unjust still; if
filthy now, it will be filthy still; if righteous now, it will be righteous still; and
if holy now, it will be holy still."

The Resurrection at Christ's Coming Will Be Universal

"Behold, I show you a mystery; We
shall not all sleep, but we shall all be

changed, in a moment, in the twinkling of an eye, at the last trump: for the trumpet shall sound, and the dead shall be raised incorruptible, and we shall be changed" (1 Cor. 15: 51, 52). No one will deny that the apostle here speaks of a resurrection that includes the church; and mark the fact that the trump which calls them forth is called the "last trump." By this we are to understand that all the dead, both righteous and wicked, will come forth at that time; for how could another trump call forth the wicked a thousand years after the "last trump" had sounded? Preposterous. The language is clear. "The trumpet ["last trump"] shall sound, and the dead [all the dead] shall be raised, . . . and we [the living] shall be changed."

"But I would not have you to be ignorant, brethren, concerning them which are asleep, that ye sorrow not, even as others which have no hope. For if we believe that Jesus died and rose

again, even so them also which sleep in
Jesus will God bring with him.   For
this we say unto you by the word of the
Lord, that we which are alive and remain unto the coming of the Lord shall
not prevent them which are asleep. For
the Lord himself shall descend from
heaven with a shout, and with the voice
of the archangel, and with the trump of
God: and the dead in Christ shall rise
first: then we which are alive and remain shall be caught up together with
them in the clouds, to meet the Lord in
the air: and so shall we ever be with
the Lord" (1 Thess. 4: 13-17).   Here
we are plainly told that the resurrection
of the dead will take place at the very
time "the Lord himself shall descend
from heaven with a shout, . . . and
with the trump of God"—the last trump.
The order of the resurrection is also
clearly given. Those that "are alive and
remain unto the coming of the Lord
shall not prevent them which are asleep.

For . . . the dead in Christ shall rise first." "The living, who are left over to the coming of the Lord, will by no means precede those who fell asleep. Because the Lord himself will come down from heaven with a shout, . . . and the dead in Christ will be raised first, then we, the living, who are left over, shall at the same time with them, be caught away in the clouds, for a meeting of the Lord in the air; and so we shall be always with the Lord."—Emphatic Diaglott. "The living who are left over unto the arrival of the Lord, in no wise may get before those who fell asleep. . . . The dead in Christ will rise first; after that, we, the living who are left over, all at once, together with them, shall be caught away, etc."—Rotherham. "We who are living, who survive to behold the appearing of our Lord, shall not enter into his presence sooner than the dead."—Conybeare and Howson. This is clear

and conclusive. The saints living on
earth when Christ comes will not "precede" the righteous dead. They will
first be raised before we enter into the
presence of the Lord. After this we,
"together with them," shall be caught
up and be forever with the Lord.

While in this scripture the apostle was
treating directly on the hope of the
church, yet the wicked are referred to
by implication in the immediate context. "For yourselves know perfectly
that the day of the Lord so cometh as a
thief in the night. . . . But ye, brethren, are not in darkness, that that day
should overtake you as a thief . . .
therefore let us not sleep, as do others;
but let us watch and be sober" (chap.
5: 2-6). When the Lord descends from
heaven with a shout, not only will the
righteous dead hear his voice, but the
wicked also will come forth at the same
time. "For the hour is coming, in the
which all that are in the graves shall

hear his voice, and shall come forth; they that have done good, unto the resurrection of life; and they that have done evil, unto the resurrection of damnation" (John 5: 28, 29). This scripture forever demolishes the theory of an intervening thousand years between the resurrection of the righteous and that of the wicked.

Christ positively declared that all that are in the graves, both "they that have done good" and "they that have done evil," shall hear his voice, and come forth in the same "hour." Daniel, looking forward with prophetic eye to the very end of time, beheld this universal resurrection, and thus described it: "And many of them that sleep in the dust of the earth shall awake, some to everlasting life, and some to shame and everlasting contempt" (Dan. 12: 2). In Young's Bible Translation this text is rendered: "And the multitude of those sleeping in the dust of the ground do awake, some to life age-during, and some to reproaches—to abhorrence age-during." Here again, is the truth that the whole multitude of the dead, both righteous and wicked, will come forth in the last day. In Paul's defense before Felix, he boldly declares "that there shall be a resurrection of the dead, both of the just and unjust" (Acts 24: 15). How many resurrections? **"A resurrection** of the dead." Who are included in that resurrection? "Both the just and unjust." So positively teaches the immutable word of truth, which liveth and abideth forever. "A resurrection there shall certainly be both of righteous and of unrighteous."—Rotherham's Translation. Could language more clearly teach but one literal resurrection, and that resurrection made up "both of righteous and unrighteous"? If Paul had believed the millennium heresy, he would have said, "There shall be two resurrections of the dead:

one of the just, the other of the unjust."
But, thank God, Paul was not of the
"simpler sort" Origen speaks of, but
spoke by inspiration of God.

The Revelator says concerning Jesus,
that when "he cometh with clouds,"
"every eye shall see him, and they also
which pierced him" (Rev. 1: 7). This
so clearly proves that both classes of
the human family will be raised at that
time, that there is no question about it.
"And I saw a great white throne, and
him that sat on it. . . . And I saw the
dead, small and great, stand before
God; and the books were opened: and
another book was opened, which is the
book of life: and the dead were judged
out of those things which were written
in the books, according to their works.
And the sea gave up the dead which
were in it; . . . and they were judged
every man according to their works.
. . . And whosoever was not found
written in the book of life was cast into

the lake of fire" (Rev. 20: 11-15). Here
we see the dead—**all the dead**—coming
forth from land and sea, and immediately following are the judgment and
the separation of the righteous and the
wicked, "and whosoever was not found
written in the book of life was cast into
the lake of fire." The language clearly
implies that in that day of final examination some will be found in the book
of life and others will not. "How say
some among you that there is no resurrection of the dead? But if there be no
resurrection of the dead, then is Christ
not risen" (1 Cor. 15: 12, 13). "For
since by man came death, by man came
also the resurrection of the dead" (v.
21). "He shall rise again in the resurrection at the last day" (John 11: 24).
Who, but such as are blinded by deception, can fail to see that in these texts
but one resurrection, the "resurrection
of the dead"—all the dead—is spoken

of, and that that resurrection will take place "at the last day"?

Christ affirms four times in one chapter that the righteous will be raised up **"at the** LAST DAY" (John 6: 39, 40, 44, 54). Martha, in speaking to Jesus concerning her dead brother said, "I know that he shall rise again in the resurrection **at the last day**" (John 11:24). Millennium teachers claim that it is the wicked who will be raised on the last day, and that the righteous will be raised one thousand years before. As there can be no days after the **last,** and the righteous will come forth on the last day, at the sounding of the "last trump," it follows that the resurrection of the dead will be universal, including both the righteous and the wicked.

The First Resurrection

While the points in this chapter have been somewhat treated in Book I of this series, it seems fitting to present them here again, for in the minds of most readers they stand associated with the preceding chapter.

"Blessed and holy is he that hath part in the first resurrection" (Rev. 20: 6). Having seen in the previous chapter that the final and universal resurrection of all the dead will take place at the instant of Christ's second advent, it follows conclusively that the resurrection here referred to as "the first resurrection" must precede his coming. If an actual resurrection takes place now, it must be the first, for it precedes in point of time the literal resurrection of either the righteous dead or the wicked. This expression "the first resurrection," in Revelation 20, may have a specific or local meaning, created by the context, referring to the exaltation of the martyrs—those who were slain for Christ's sake were caught up to God and his throne. All these were "blessed and holy"; but it is certain that they had had part in a spiritual resurrection. But do the Scriptures teach such a resurrection? Yes. John says, "We know that we have passed from death unto life" (1 John 3:14). This is clear. First. An actual resurrection now takes place: men pass from "death unto life." Second. This resurrection is spiritual, and makes men "blessed and holy." Be assured, dear reader, that the writer is one that "hath part in the first resurrection."

"But," says one, "there can be no resurrection except there first be a death." This is true; but death reigns on every hand. Every unregenerated man and woman is dead, spiritually dead—"dead in trespasses and sins" (Eph. 2:1). "We were dead in sins" (v. 5). "You being dead in your sins" (Col. 2:13). "To be carnally minded is death" (Rom. 8:6). "The soul that sinneth, it shall die" (Ezek. 18:4). "Sin, when it is fin-

ished, bringeth forth death" (Jas. 1:
15). "Sin revived, and I died" (Rom.
7:9). "She that liveth in pleasure is
dead while she liveth" (1 Tim. 5:6).
"He that loveth not his brother abideth
in death" (1 John 3:14). When God
forbade our foreparents to eat of the
tree of knowledge of good and evil, he
told them, "In the day that thou eatest
thereof thou shalt surely die." They
transgressed, a n d death — spiritual
death—was the immediate result. It is
true that physical death was entailed on
the race by this first transgression, but
it is none the less true that thereby man
died spiritually. And this spiritual
death did not stop with Adam. The
effects of the fall were far-reaching. The
whole human family were plunged into
death, as the result of Adam's sin. "By
one man [Adam] sin entered into the
world, and death by sin; and so death
passed upon all men, for that all have
sinned" (Rom. 5:12). Again, we read

that "death reigned from Adam to Moses" (v. 14). The word "death" in these texts clearly refers to spiritual death in trespasses and sins.

Spiritual death reigned from Adam to Moses. Then Moses gave a law, but it was too weak to give life. Paul says, "If there had been a law given which could have given life, verily righteousness should have been by the law" (Gal. 3:21). Spiritual life, then, could not be obtained by the law. So it is a positive fact that spiritual death reigned over the world from Adam to Christ. Death was God's decree upon fallen man. Oh, the misery and woe that followed in its trail! But while death was reigning, and the millions of earth were in slumber, the sweet accents of the gospel reverberated throughout the length and breadth of the earth, bringing to its despairing myriads the comforting message that Christ "hath abolished death, and hath brought life and immortality to light through the gospel" (2 Tim. 1:10). "I am come that they might have life" (John 10:10). "Wherefore he saith, Awake, thou that sleepest, and arise from the dead, and Christ shall give thee light" (Eph. 5: 14). Amen.

The first resurrection began with this gospel dispensation. Surely no one will deny that the spiritual work of God in our souls is a real and very important resurrection. The loud blast from the trumpet of truth to fallen man in this dispensation is: "Awake, thou that sleepest, and arise from the dead." Jesus said, "I am the resurrection and the life: he that believeth in me, though he were dead, yet shall he live: and whosoever liveth and believeth in me shall never die" (John 11: 25, 26). "Verily, verily, I say unto you, he that heareth my word, and believeth on him that sent me, hath everlasting life, and shall not come into condemnation; but is passed from death unto life. Verily, verily, I say unto you, the hour is coming, and now is, when the dead shall hear the voice of the Son of God; and they that hear shall live" (John 5: 24, 25). Need anything be plainer than this?

The first resurrection is spiritual. It is progressive, or a continuous operation throughout the gospel era. It was then present, and yet to come. It is personal and conditional. "The dead shall hear the voice of the Son of God, and they that hear shall live"; that is, they that hear with acceptance of the same. Again, those who receive this resurrection are justified from all their sins, and "shall not come into condemnation, but are passed from death unto life." We shall next give examples of those who had attained unto this resurrection.

Paul exhorted the Roman brethren: "Yield yourselves unto God, as those that are alive from the dead" (Rom. 6: 13). "And you hath he quickened,

who were dead in trespasses and sins."
"Even when we were dead in sins, hath
quickened us together with Christ, (by
grace ye are saved;) and hath raised
us up together" (Eph. 2: 1, 5, 6). "And
you, being dead in your sins and the
uncircumcision of your flesh, hath he
quickened together with him, having
forgiven you all trespasses" (Col. 2:
13). "Ye are risen with him" (v. 12).
"If ye then be risen with Christ, seek
those things which are above" (3: 1).
"We know that we have passed from
death unto life" (1 John 3: 14). The
following undeniable facts are clearly
set forth in the foregoing scriptures.
First, all sinners are dead in trespasses
and sins; second, all such are commanded to awake out of sleep and "arise
from the dead"; third, when men and
women get saved in Christ, an actual
resurrection takes place; fourth, this
resurrection makes men "blessed and
holy"; fifth, being an actual resurrec-

tion, and antedating all others, it must of necessity be the first.

While the millions quickened to life throughout this entire gospel dispensation all taken together compose the "first resurrection," it may properly be said that in an important sense there have been two spiritual resurrections; namely, the mighty host raised up before the "Dark Ages," and the second host saved since that time. Through the pure gospel of the primitive church, a large host of souls were raised from death unto life. They were "a royal priesthood," "a holy nation." They reigned "in life" over Satan, sin, and the world. But soon the darkness of the apostasy crushed out the light of God. "What are termed the Middle Ages commenced with the fifth, and terminated with the fifteenth century. Of these the first six are denominated the Dark Ages; but throughout the whole period, Christianity suffered a long eclipse of a thousand years."—Goodrich's Church History, p. 478. During that dark period salvation work, with a few exceptions, ceased; and the "rest of the dead" of Adam's fallen race "lived not again until the thousand years were finished." The kingdom of God was largely hid under the human rubbish of men. The reign on earth ceased, and the only reign enjoyed by the people of God was enjoyed "with Christ" in paradise by that host who had taken part in the first resurrection. But the Reformation again brings the resurrecting grace of God into action, and thousands of the "rest of the dead" have been, and are being, made alive in Christ. Hallelujah! (See Rev. 20: 4-6.)

"Some to Everlasting Life"

We have seen that, in the general resurrection at the last day, "they that have done good" shall come forth "unto the resurrection of life." On this point Daniel informs us that "many of them that sleep in the dust of the earth shall awake, **some to everlasting life.**" This implies a resurrection in an immortal, glorified body, unto an eternal reward. Paul speaks with direct reference to this point when he says, "that I may know him, and the power of his resurrection, and the fellowship of his sufferings, being made conformable unto his death; if by any means I might attain unto the resurrection of the dead. Not as though I had already attained, either were already perfect; but I follow after, if that I may apprehend that for which also I am apprehended of Christ Jesus. Brethren, I count not myself to have apprehended: but this one thing I do, forgetting those things which are behind, and reaching forth unto those things which are before, I press toward the mark for the prize of the high calling of God in Christ Jesus" (Phil. 3: 10-14).

The resurrection from the dead was a perfection Paul had not yet attained. His object in life was to live in such a manner that he might attain "unto the resurrection of the dead." By this he makes clear that it is not merely a part in the general resurrection he desires, for all the dead shall be raised, but a resurrection unto eternal life; a resurrection in which his vile body shall be changed and "fashioned like unto His glorious body" (v. 21); a resurrection unto eternal rewards, when "the prize of the high calling of God in Christ Jesus" shall be eternally his. This resurrection unto eternal life is termed "the resurrection of the just." It is also termed "the redemption of our body" (Rom. 8: 23). "For the trumpet shall sound, and the dead shall be raised incorruptible, and we [the living] shall be changed. . . . For this corruptible

must put on incorruption, and this mortal must put on immortality. So when
this corruptible shall have put on incorruption, and this mortal shall have put
on immortality, then shall be brought
to pass the saying that is written, Death
is swallowed up in victory. O death,
where is thy sting? O grave, where is
thy victory? The sting of death is sin;
and the strength of sin is the law. But
thanks be to God, which giveth us the
victory through our Lord Jesus Christ"
(1 Cor. 15: 52-57). This describes the
glories of the future resurrection of the
redeemed, and a time when death will
be swallowed up in victory.

The numberless myriads of them
"that are Christ's at his coming" will
come forth at the trumpet sound, robed
in the garments of righteousness and
eternal glory, to be caught up for a
meeting of the Lord in the air, and "so
shall we ever be with the Lord." What
an inspiring thought! What a morning

that will be! The long night of silent
slumber in the grave will be suddenly
broken by the peal of the trumpet and
the shout of Jehovah, and at the sound
of that trump and voice, the graves will
burst open, and even the sea shall give
up the dead which is in it.

Such a morning will never before be
known as the resurrection will be to the
redeemed millions. "Weeping may endure for the night, but joy cometh in
the morning." "The shadows had gathered, the stars had become beclouded,
the rain was falling, the winds were
blowing aloof, night and clouds and
weeping, fainting, senselessness—and
then, morning! We shall wake in light
and warmth and health. We shall see
the skies of eternity, we shall breathe
the airs of paradise, we shall feel the
vigor of immortality, we shall hear the
voices of heaven—sweet voices, mu-
sical, transporting, as the sound as of
many waters, voices attuned to our con-

dition, mingling old familiar words and tunes with tones and cadences that could come only from hearts sweet with heaven, and through throats and mouths that had long breathed the air of heaven. Perhaps they may make us happy with a song of assurance which once drew tears from our eyes as a song of hope:

> 'Here is rest for the weary,
> Here is rest for the weary,
>   Here is rest for you.
> On this morning side of Jordan,
> In these sweet fields of Eden,
> Where the tree of Life is blooming,
>   Here is rest for you.'

"Can we refrain? Shall we not join them? Shall we not go with them? Shall we not quickly learn to sing the 'song of Moses and the Lamb,' the song of everlasting law and everlasting love? Shall we not see and hear and join the 'great voice of much people in heaven, saying, Alleluia! Salvation, and glory, and honor, and power, unto the Lord our God'? It is morning! Hark! 'The voice of a great multitude, and as the voice of many waters, and as the voice of mighty thunderings, saying, Alleluia: for the Lord God Omnipotent reigneth.' We join that throng, we join that song. Where is weeping now? Fled with the night. He has wiped all tears from all eyes. O softest hand of everlasting love! O eyes forever brightened by the benediction of the touch of the Lord! O morning, cloudless, tearless, brilliant, balmy, and everlasting! O men, O brothers, bear the weeping! The night is short. The morning comes. In the night weeping is a lodger, in the morning joy is an everlasting mate.

> 'Brief life is here our portion,
>   Brief sorrow, short-lived care;
> The life that knows no ending,
>   The tearless life is there.
> And now we fight the battle,
>   And then shall wear the crown
> Of full and everlasting
>   And passionless renown.'

"Break, O Morning, break on the

souls that are in the night of sin; and
on our graves, break, O Morning of the
Everlasting Day!"

"Some to Shame and Everlasting Contempt"

While most of the teaching of the Bible on the subject of the resurrection
has direct and special reference to the
future hope of the church, yet a number
of texts clearly teach that the wicked
also will be raised. "All that are in the
graves shall hear his voice, and shall
come forth, . . . they that have done
evil, unto the resurrection of damnation"; or, as Daniel words it, "some to
shame and everlasting contempt." Of
the resurrected bodies of the unbeliev-
ers, the Scriptures apparently are silent.
But from the fact that theirs is a resurrection to **"eternal** damnation," we may
infer that they also will come forth with

immortal bodies. This is also evident
from the fact that with the universal
resurrection of all the dead, death itself—the last enemy—shall be destroyed. "The trumpet shall sound, and
the dead [all the dead] shall be raised
incorruptible, and we shall be changed."
What a contrast between their coming
forth and that of the righteous! The
latter will be to eternal rewards amid
the glories of heaven, and the former
to shame and everlasting contempt.

Concerning the bodies of the wicked
in the resurrection, I quote the following from T. Dewitt Talmage:

"It is probable that as the wicked are,
in the last day, to be opposite in character, so will they be, in many respects
opposite in body. As the bodies of the
righteous are glorious—those of the
wicked will be repelling. You know
how bad passions flatten the skull and
disfigure the body. There he comes!
up out of the graveyard—the drunk-

ard; the blotches on his body flaming out in worse disfigurement, and his tongue bitten by an all-consuming thirst for drink—which he can not get, for there are no dram-shops in hell. There comes up the lascivious and unclean wretch, reeking with filth that made him the horror of the city hospital, now wriggling across the cemetery lots—the consternation of devils. Here are all the faces of the unpardoned dead. The last line of attractiveness is dashed out, and the eye is wild, malignant, fierce, infernal; the cheek aflame; the mouth distorted with blasphemies. If the glance of the faces of the righteous was like a new morning, the glance of the faces of the lost will be like another night falling on midnight. If, after the close of a night's debauch, a man gets up and sits on the side of the bed—sick, exhausted, and horrified with a review of his past; or rouses up in delirium tremens, and sees serpents crawling over

him, or devils dancing about him—
what will be the feeling of a man who
gets up out of his bed on the last morning of earth, and reviews an unpardoned
past, and, instead of imaginary evils
crawling over him and flitting before
him, finds the real frights and pains and
woes of the resurrection of damnation?"

The General Judgment

"And Enoch also, the seventh from
Adam, prophesied of these, saying, Behold, the Lord cometh with ten thousands of his saints, to execute judgment
upon all, and to convince all that are
ungodly among them of all their ungodly deeds which they have ungodly
committed, and of all their hard
speeches which ungodly sinners have
spoken against him" (Jude 14:15).
"Wherein they think it strange that ye

run not with them to the same excess
of riot, speaking evil of you: who shall
give account to him that is ready to
judge the quick and the dead" (1 Pet.
4: 4, 5). "I charge thee therefore before God, and the Lord Jesus Christ,
who shall judge the quick and the dead
at his appearing and kingdom" (2 Tim.
4: 1). Thank God for this clear testimony!

Instead of Christ's setting up a millennial kingdom at his appearing, it is
positively declared that he will judge
the "quick" (the living, who will be
changed) and the "dead" (those raised
from their graves). It is not a thousand
years after he comes that the general
judgment will take place, but at the
very time of his appearing. "Therefore
judge nothing before the time, until the
Lord come, who both will bring to light
the hidden things of darkness and will
make manifest the counsels of the
hearts" (1 Cor. 4: 5). "But after thy

hardness and impenitent heart treasurest up unto thyself wrath against the
day of wrath and revelation of the righteous judgment of God; who will render
to every man according to his deeds"
(Rom. 2: 5, 6).

That a millennial age will follow
Christ's second coming is utterly un-
scriptural.   The revelation of Jesus
Christ from heaven will be the time of
the general judgment, the reward of the
righteous, and the perdition of the ungodly.   1 Cor. 4: 5 clearly proves that
the judgment will take place 'when the
Lord comes.' Rom. 2: 4-6 is a solemn
warning to ungodly men who oppose
the truth and presume upon God's
mercies. To such, the revelation of Jesus Christ from heaven will be a day of
wrath, when God shall "render to every
man according to his deeds."

Most millennium teachers claim that
the righteous will not be included in
this final and general judgment.   But

their teaching stands in square contradiction to the apostle's, for he boldly asserts that "we shall all stand before the judgment-seat of Christ. For it is written, As I live, saith the Lord, every knee shall bow to me, and every tongue shall confess to God. So then **every one of us** shall give an account of himself to God" (Rom. 14: 10-12). "For we must all appear before the judgment-seat of Christ; that every one may receive the things done in his body, according to that he hath done, whether it be good or bad. Knowing therefore the terror of the Lord, we persuade men" (2 Cor. 5: 10, 11). Thank God for the hammer of truth, which demolishes every false doctrine! How clear this testimony! The dead—all the dead —"small and great," "good and bad," **"shall all** stand before the judgment-seat of Christ" in that great day. Yes, dear reader, whether saved or unsaved, "we must **all** appear before the judgment-seat of Christ." And then, says the apostle, "every one of us shall give account of himself to God"; "that every one may receive the things done in his body, according to that he hath done, whether it be **good or bad**."

Nature of the Judgment

Jesus, in speaking of the prince of this world—the devil—being cast out, said, "Now is the judgment of this world" (John 12: 31). He also said, "For judgment I am come into this world, that they which see not might see, and that they which see might be made blind" (John 9: 39). The Father gave him "authority to execute judgment also, because he is the Son of man" (John 5: 27). These texts have reference to Christ's exercising his authority and power against Satan and sin during the present dispensation. The gospel of the kingdom that he preached during his incarnation was judgment, and it broke the Satanic chains of darkness, which had held fast the world for long ages.

In this present time the saints have the honor to execute "the judgment written" (see Psa. 149: 5-9). And in 1 Pet. 4: 17 it is said that "the time is come that judgment must begin at the house of God: and if it first begin at us, what shall the end be of them that obey not the gospel of God?" These texts, with many others, teach that a preliminary judgment is sweeping over the earth at the present time. It is effected through the preaching of the pure gospel by the power of the Holy Spirit. The spirit of judgment and the spirit of burning were to be characteristic of the church of God, especially in the last days of the Christian era. Zion was to be "redeemed with judgment, and her converts with righteousness." Some

have supposed that this is all the judgment that will ever take place. It is
true that the clear teaching of the word
of God draws a line of demarcation between those who serve God and those
who do not, and thus the people of earth
are now, in a sense, brought into the valley of judgment, and into the valley of
decision, and their future destiny is
sealed by their acceptance or rejection
of the truth; yet this does not conflict
in the least with the fact of a future
judgment, or, as Paul terms it, the
"judgment to come" (Acts 24: 25).
There is an **appointed day** of judgment—"He hath appointed a day, in
the which he will judge the world in
righteousness by that man whom he
hath ordained; whereof he hath given
assurance unto all men, in that he hath
raised him from the dead" (Acts 17:
31). The general judgment of the last
day is an event to follow death, hence
it is future—"It is appointed unto men

once to die, but after this the judgment"
(Heb. 9: 27).

While the teeming millions of all
ages will be summoned before the great
tribunal, yet there will be an individual
sense in which "every one of us shall
give an account of himself to God."
Every one must stand or fall on his own
merits. A fair trial will be given to
each one, but not one shall escape that
judgment. It may be possible to cover
up sin and crime in this world, as many
do, but all will be uncovered in that
great day. Each one will be conscious
of the all-piercing eye of the omniscient
God. "For God shall bring every work
into judgment, with every secret thing,
whether it be good, or whether it be
evil" (Eccl. 12: 14).

"The judgment will be a scene of
extraordinary interest to saints, angels,
and devils. All these classes of intelli-
gences shall be there." The glorified
saints will be present, as appears from

what is said in Rev. 11 : 18: "Thy wrath
is come, and the time of the dead, that
they should be judged, and that thou
shouldest give reward unto thy servants
the prophets, and to the saints, and
them that fear thy name, small and
great." This text proves that the day
of judgment will be the day of God's
wrath upon the ungodly, and also the
day of reward to the saints. There is
not the slightest hint of a thousand
years' reign, or of any offers of salvation to be given to any one, after the
ushering in of that great and notable
day of the Lord.

It is evident that Satan, who is the
prince of devils, and all his host, look
forward to the judgment with anxious
foreboding. Jesus informs us that the
everlasting fires of hell were prepared
for them. The Bible also clearly states
that the devil himself shall be cast into
the lake of fire and brimstone. That
these demons are aware of the doom

that awaits them is clear from the conversation Jesus had with the legion confronting him at the tombs. "And, behold, they cried out, saying, What have we to do with thee, Jesus, thou Son of God? art thou come hither to torment us before the time?" (Matt. 8:29). From this it appears that a greater degree of punishment awaits the devils than they have yet endured, and that they know there is a time determined by the divine Judge when they will be sent into greater torments. It seems they are well acquainted with the great doctrine of Christ's coming in the glory of the Father, with all his holy angels. Hence their consternation at meeting him so unexpectedly and in such a manner. These devils well knew that the time was coming when they would be cast into the bottomless pit, but they also knew that the time had not yet arrived; and they seemed to dread the presence of Christ lest they should ex-

perience the agony of everlasting burnings before their time.

The Bible is full of warning and exhortation with reference to this great
and eventful day. It portrays to us the
terrors of the wicked as they seek for
death and find it not. Then will the
prophecy of the wise man reach an
awful fulfilment—"Because I have
called and ye refused; I have stretched
out my hand and no man regarded; but
ye have set at nought all my counsel,
and would none of my reproof: I also
will laugh at your calamity; I will mock
when your fear cometh; when your fear
cometh as desolation, and your destruction cometh as a whirlwind; when distress and anguish cometh upon you.
Then shall they call upon me, but I will
not answer; they shall seek me early,
but they shall not find me: for that they
hated knowledge and did not choose the
fear of the Lord: They would none of
my counsel; they despised all my re-

proof: therefore shall they eat of the fruit of their own way, and be filled with their own devices" (Prov. 1: 24-31).

Necessity of the Judgment

'According to the Bible, the final judgment has in view the following objects: To convince the ungodly of the justice of their doom (Jude 14, 15); to make a general and grand impression upon the intelligent universe of the perfect righteousness of God in making an eternal distinction in the final allotment of the righteous and the wicked. Christ taught this object of the judgment as recorded in Matt. 25: 31-46. Now, obviously both these ends are best secured by a general judgment in which the case of each class is investigated and decided, at which the countless hosts of all the intelligent beings in the

universe of God are present. Oh, it will
be an august day!'

Since final reward and punishment
follow the judgment, the need of such
a day of trial and reckoning is made
clear. A similar order is followed in
the courts of our land today. When a
crime is committed, enlightened citi-
zens do not believe in lynching the criminal, but he is arrested and put in prison,
where he is held over for trial. On a
certain stated day he is arraigned before the judge, the evidences are given
in, and if he is proved innocent, he is
acquitted; but if he is proved guilty, he
is sentenced to be punished. So with
God's arraignment. Death, like an of-
ficer, arrests us. Next we pass into the
intermediate world of spirits—the righteous to paradise, where they rest from
their labors in bright anticipation of
their future eternal reward to be given
at the judgment; the wicked to chains
of darkness and pits of gloom, reserved

"unto the day of judgment to be punished" (2 Pet. 2: 4, 9). They are like prisoners awaiting trial who already know that the evidences are all against them. Having closed their lives in rebellion against the throne of God, with "a fearful looking for of judgment and fiery indignation," knowing that it is a "fearful thing to fall into the hands of the living God," they are already in a state of awful torment in the intermediate state. Like the rich man in Hades, they are tormented by the flames of a guilty conscience.

A day of judgment has been appointed, when all shall be summoned before the august presence of the great Judge of all the earth, and when reward and punishment will be meted out according to the deeds done in the body. The works and influences set in motion during our lifetime here continue to live after we are dead. For example: the life and teachings of Paul have an

earthly immortality that is influencing
thousands and millions of people during all the centuries of the Christian era.
Thus he sowed in time and will reap in
eternity.   Full reward could not be
given at death, for his influence for good
still lives, and his reward shall be "according to his works." So with each one
of us.   I shall not be rewarded merely
for what I do while I live, but for the
accomplishments of the influences I set
in motion in life, which will live and
work for good after my departure. This
should be an inspiring thought to Christians who have not the opportunities to
accomplish much in a visible way while
they live.

The Christian mother with a large
family of children, who is daily bur-
dened with cares and responsibilities,
has many discouragements that others
know little about.   Sometimes she is
tempted to think that her life of drudg-
ery and hard work is simply spent in

vain. She lives, nevertheless, a prayer-
ful, devoted life to God, and sets a godly example before her children. Often
in the still hours of the night she pours
out her heart to God for the salvation
of her sons and daughters. She does
her best to instruct them in the ways of
the Lord. But it seems with all her
efforts they continue in sin. Finally she
dies without realizing her hope in seeing her children brought to Christ. But
she has left to her family the legacy of
a mother's prayers, a holy life, and a
Christian example. She 'rests from her
labors, and her works do follow her.'
Ere long that wayward boy, like the
prodigal, comes to himself. Something
is brought to bear upon him that awak-
ens in him a realization of the utter
folly of a sinful life and the profitable-
ness of serving God. As these thoughts
fill his mind, memory goes back to child-
hood's gleeful hours spent at Mother's
knee, and his boyhood days around the

family fireside at home. Mother's godly example and life and earnest prayers
come before him, and with tears stream-
ing down his cheeks, and with penitent
soul, he cries, "Mother's God and religion shall be mine!" In that man's
heart and mind lie talents that will perhaps shake the world. These have long
lain dormant or have been exercised in
a wrong direction. Now he consecrates
them to the service of God. The result
is, many are brought to the light, and
in turn still more, whose influence and
work continue to widen until time ends.
But where did this mighty stream start?
What was the spring from which it
emanated? Answer. The meek and
quiet Christian life of a saintly mother
in her home. In the day of judgment
that mother will see sheaves of golden
grain brought into the great heavenly
store, as the result of the life that she
lived. This will add greatly to her
crown of rejoicing. It also shows the

necessity of a future judgment and day of awards.

The disorders of society require that there be a future judgment. There are disorders which strike the senses, astonish reason, and subvert faith itself; yet these things go on unpunished. Many times the innocent suffer and the guilty go free. Human laws often fail to mete out justice; in fact, right judgment is sometimes perverted and the wrong triumphs. All this demands a final reckoning, when just judgment will be meted out to all.

The oppression of the poor by the rich and arrogant necessitates a future judgment. And in view of this fact, James assures us that the cries of the oppressed of earth have "entered the ears of the Lord of sabaoth." He also says, "Be patient therefore, brethren, unto the coming of the Lord"; "Be ye also patient; stablish your hearts: for the coming of the Lord draweth nigh."

That will be a day when justice will be meted out to those who have "condemned and killed the just," a day when rich men will 'weep and howl, for the miseries that shall come upon them' (Jas. 5: 1-8).

Our attitude toward those who persecute and maltreat us is to be one of love, forbearance, and endurance, with this assurance, "Vengeance is mine; I will repay, saith the Lord." God's people have always been a persecuted people. Millions of them, during the Dark Ages, "were slain for the word of God, and for the testimony which they held." But a day is coming when God will judge and avenge their blood on them that dwell on the earth (see Rev. 6: 8-10). Thus again we see the necessity of the judgment.

With this very thought in mind, Paul says: "So that we ourselves glory in you in the churches of God, for your patience and faith in all your persecu-

tions and tribulations that ye endure;
which is a manifest token of the righteous judgment of God, that ye may be
counted worthy of the kingdom of God,
for which ye also suffer: seeing it is a
righteous thing with God to recompense
tribulation to them that trouble you;
and to you who are troubled, rest with
us, when the Lord Jesus shall be revealed from heaven with his mighty
angels, in flaming fire taking vengeance
on them that know not God, and that
obey not the gospel of our Lord Jesus
Christ: who shall be punished" (2
Thess. 1: 4-9).

The words of the apostle are certainly to be understood as teaching that
the sufferings of the just and the triumphs of the wicked in this life, are a
sure proof that there will be a future
judgment in which the wicked shall be
punished and the righteous rewarded.

Description of the Final Judgment

Jesus, in all the dignity and splendor of his eternal majesty, will descend from heaven, and "then shall he sit upon the throne of his glory; and before him shall be gathered all nations; and he shall separate them one from another, as a shepherd divideth his sheep from the goats" (Matt. 25:31, 32). "I beheld till the thrones were cast down, and the Ancient of days did sit, whose garment was white as snow, and the hair of his head like the pure wool: his throne was like the fiery flame, and his wheels as burning fire. A fiery stream issued and came forth from before him: thousand thousands ministered unto him, and ten thousand times ten thousand stood before him: the judgment was set, and the books were opened" (Dan. 7:9, 10). "And I saw a great white throne, and him that sat on it, from whose face the earth and heaven fled away; and there was found no place for them. And I saw the dead, small and great, stand before God: and the books were opened; and another book was opened, which is the book of life: and the dead were judged out of those things which were written in the books, according to their works" (Rev. 20: 11, 12).

It would seem that the foregoing description of the final day of judgment is so plain that comment is unnecessary. There is absolutely no intimation of a literal kingdom being established and a reign of a thousand years on earth being inaugurated. No offers of salvation are given. With the lightning flash and pealing thunders of Christ's coming, instantly appears the great white throne of his glory, and before him is gathered all nations. The dead, small and great, shall then stand before God. That is, they shall stand before the throne of his judgment. This throne

is described as a "great white throne,"
and "like a fiery flame." Paul no doubt
speaks of the same thing when he says
that the Lord Jesus "shall be revealed
from heaven . . . in FLAMING FIRE."
What a sight this will be to the millions
of the unsaved who will stand on the
left side of the great Judge in that awful day of final wrath! What an inspiring sight to the hosts of redeemed ones
who will be gathered on the right side
to hear the Master say, "Come ye blessed, inherit the kingdom."

The Great Gathering

"Now we beseech you, brethren, by
the coming of our Lord Jesus Christ,
and by our gathering together unto him"
(2 Thess. 2: 1). This great gathering
is doubtless the same as the one Paul
speaks of in 1 Thess. 4: 16, 17: "For
the Lord himself shall descend from

heaven with a shout; . . . then we which are alive and remain, shall be caught up together with them [the dead in Christ who have just been raised] in the clouds, to meet the Lord in the air: and so shall we ever be with the Lord." Not only will the righteous be gathered before the great white throne of judgment, but the wicked also; for Jesus says, "When the Son of man shall come in his glory, and all the holy angels with him, then shall he sit upon the throne of his glory: and before him shall be gathered **all nations;** and he shall separate them one from another, as a shepherd divideth his sheep from the goats" (Matt. 25: 31, 32).

What a gathering that will be! From every cemetery, and even from the depths of the sea, all around the world, the dead will come forth and will be gathered to one place—the place of judgment—before the great white throne.

Note the fact that in almost every text referring to Christ's coming, it is said that the angels shall accompany him. These angels now wait upon the Lord in heaven and are his ministering spirits. And it is very clear from the testimony of Scripture that they will assist him in the great work of gathering and separating the nations of earth. In Matt. 24: 30, 31, we read that when the Son of man shall come "in the clouds of heaven, with power and great glory, he shall send his angels with a great sound of a trumpet; and they shall gather together his elect from the four winds, from one end of heaven to the other." This gathering together is directly associated with Christ's coming. This fact is made very clear from the language of Jesus as recorded in Mark 13: 26, 27—"And then shall they see the Son of man coming in the clouds, with great power and glory; **and then** shall he send his angels, and shall gather together his elect from the four winds, from the uttermost parts of the earth to the uttermost part of heaven."

Myriads of angels shall accompany him, and go forth "from the uttermost part of the earth to the uttermost part of heaven," and gather before him all nations; in other words, every intelligent creature. What a concourse that will be! There have been great assemblages at different periods in the history of time, but such a gathering as this never has been. All the host of heaven, as well as the multitudes of earth, will be gathered there.

Friend, think of this. You can not escape it. You can not evade it. "We shall ALL appear before the judgment seat of Christ." When all mankind is thus gathered before the great white throne, it is said, "he shall separate them the one from another, as a shepherd divideth his sheep from the goats." The angels will assist in this work, the

same as in the gathering. "So shall it
be in the end of the world. The Son of
man shall send forth his angels, and
they shall gather out of his kingdom all
things that offend, and them which do
iniquity, and shall cast them into a furnace of fire: there shall be wailing and
gnashing of teeth. Then shall the
righteous shine forth as the sun in the
kingdom of their Father" (Matt. 13:
40-43). "So shall it be at the end of
the world: the angels shall come forth,
and sever the wicked from among the
just; and shall cast them into the furnace of fire: there shall be wailing and
gnashing of teeth" (vs. 49, 50).

Christ the Judge

Note this fact, that in the multitude
of scriptures bearing directly on the
coming day of judgment, it is always
said that it is Christ who will appear:

we must "stand before the Son of man";
"the judgment-seat of Christ." From
this we understand that Christ will be
the Judge. This truth is confirmed by
the many direct scriptures that bear on
the point. "For the Father judgeth no
man, but hath committed all judgment
unto the Son" (John 5: 22). God will
judge the world by that man whom he
hath ordained, Christ Jesus (Acts 17:
31). "The Lord Jesus Christ, who shall
judge the quick and the dead at his appearing and kingdom" (2 Tim. 4: 1).
"And he commanded us to preach unto
the people, and to testify that it is he
which was ordained of God to be the
Judge of quick and dead" (Acts 10:42).

Since the kingdom of grace and the
great redemptive reign established during the Christian era for the salvation
of a lost world is Christ's, it is fitting
that its termination in the final judgment should rest upon his shoulders. It
is his blood that redeems the millions

who will then be rewarded. It is Christ and his reign against whom the wicked and rebellious of earth have lifted up their puny arm. He now stands in the attitude of a Savior and Redeemer for all mankind. But the millions who reject him and trample his blood beneath their feet must stand before him and give an account to him as their judge. He will be their disposer in that final day of reckoning.

O friend, today Christ is your Savior. Accept him. Believe on him. Crown him in your heart and life. "Kiss the Son, lest he be angry with you." "Today if ye will hear his voice, harden not your heart." Yes, **now** is the accepted time; behold, **now** is the day of salvation." Yes, today, **today,** Christ is your Savior. Tomorrow he will be your judge.

The Standard of Judgment

In this world today people are judged by many standards: good or bad, right or wrong. The creeds, teachings, and doctrines of men are held up as standards for people to measure to. God has but one general standard—the revealed word. The only way to have God's approval, then, is to live in perfect harmony with his revealed will. To knowingly do what it forbids, or to refuse to do what it enjoins, is sin. "For sin is the transgression of the law." This will be the general standard of judgment in the last day. Jesus makes this clear in John 12: 48: "He that rejecteth me, and receiveth not my words, hath one that judgeth him: the word that I have spoken, the same shall judge him in the last day." By referring to Rom. 2: 12-16 we learn that those who "have sinned in the law [have had a divine revelation], shall be judged by

the law; . . . in the day when God
shall judge the secrets of men, by Jesus
Christ, **according to my gospel**"; while
the heathen "which have not the law"
(no objective revelation) will be judged
by the moral law written in their hearts,
the law of conscience.

THERE WILL BE NO APPEAL FROM THIS JUDGMENT

Since the Father has committed all
judgment to the Son, there will be no
appeal from the decision rendered in
the last great day. There will be no
higher court. In Christ is hid all the
treasures of wisdom and knowledge.
He possesses all the attributes of his
Father, therefore is fully capable of
rendering a just decision. 'Before him
every knee shall bow and every tongue
shall confess.' He is exalted far above
all principality and power, and every
name that is named, both in this world
and that which is to come. "Shall not

the Judge of all the earth do right?"
It is before the **Son of man,** as well as
the Son of God, that we shall appear.
He can not but judge righteously from
the nature of his being. But, reader,
take warning. He is infinitely holy,
hence infinitely opposed to sin; and no
man with the least stain of sin can
stand in the presence of his glory un-
condemned. In view of this fact, "what
manner of persons ought ye to be in all
holy conversation and godliness?"

The standard by which he will judge
all men is his holy, just, and good law.
Every sinner will stand in the attitude
of a transgressor of this infinite and
eternal law. From this we must conclude that the decision rendered will be
final, from which there can be no appeal.

The Righteous Rewarded and the Wicked Punished

"For what is a man profited, if he shall gain the whole world, and lose his own soul? or what shall a man give in exchange for his soul? For the Son of man shall come in the glory of his Father with his angels; and then he shall reward every man according to his works" (Matt. 16: 26, 27). "Behold, I come quickly; and my reward is with me, to give every man according as his works shall be. He that is unjust, let him be unjust still: and he that is filthy, let him be filthy still: and he that is righteous, let him be righteous still: and he that is holy, let him be holy still" (Rev. 22: 12, 11). These texts are a blast of warning to all men. Christ will come in the glory of his Father, "and then [at that time] he shall reward every man according to his works," and there will be no more es-

cape from sin, but the wicked will have
forever lost their souls. We have suf-
ficiently proved that the moment of
Christ's coming will be the time of the
general resurrection of the dead, followed immediately by the general judgment, at which time "he shall reward
every man according to his works." The
revelation of Jesus Christ from heaven
will be a day of wrath, when God will
render "to every man according to his
deeds." The instant of Christ's coming
will eternally fix the fate of all men,
whether pure or sinful. The fact that
all, both righteous and wicked, will be
judged at the same time is fatal to mil-
lenarianism. But such is the plain testimony of Scripture. All the dead,
small and great, will stand at the same
time before the throne of judgment, and
whosoever is not found written in the
book of life, will be cast into the lake
of fire (Rev. 20: 12-15). This proves
that in the final examination some will

be found in the book of life and others not.

"When the Lord Jesus shall be revealed from heaven with his mighty angels, in flaming fire taking vengeance on them that know not God, and that obey not the gospel of our Lord Jesus Christ: who shall be punished with everlasting destruction from the presence of the Lord, and from the glory of his power; when he shall come to be glorified in his saints, and to be admired in all them that believe . . . in that day" (2 Thess. 1: 7-10). This text also clearly proves that both the punishment of the wicked and the reward of the righteous will be given "when the Lord Jesus will be revealed from heaven." Instead of setting up a kingdom and reigning a thousand years here upon earth for the conversion of the millions who in life rejected his offered mercies, he will come "in flaming fire taking vengeance on them that know not God, and that obey not the gospel of our Lord Jesus Christ." And mark the fact, that all this will take place "when he shall come to be glorified in his saints, and to be admired in all them that believe." Thus the rewarding of the righteous and the punishing of the wicked will take place at the same time —the time of Christ's coming—positively asserts the Word of God. Whosoever teaches to the contrary contradicts these scriptures and the many other texts already cited. Let God be true, though every opposing theory be proved false.

In different places it is said that Christ will come "with power and great glory," the "glory of the Father." This awful glory is what will drive the wicked in everlasting destruction from his presence to the flames of eternal hell. No one can enjoy the fellowship and companionship of the Creator, except those who live upon the plane of his nature and possess his holiness in this life. How, then, can any soul with the smallest spot of sin hope to stand before God in the awful day of his coming and judgment? Oh, how many plain and solemn warnings God has given to all men of that day when all must either stand or fall in the presence of his majesty and glory!

"For if God spared not the angels that sinned, but cast them down to hell, and delivered them into chains of darkness, to be reserved unto judgment; and spared not the old world, but saved Noah the eighth person, a preacher of righteousness, bringing in the flood upon the world of the ungodly; and turning the cities of Sodom and Gomorrah into ashes condemned them with an overthrow, making them an example unto those that after should live ungodly; . . . the Lord knoweth how to deliver the godly out of temptations, and to reserve the unjust unto the day of judgment to be punished" (2 Pet. 2: 4-9).

Is it not astonishing that men, in the light of such scripture as this, can become so subverted as to teach that Christ will come and set up a literal kingdom, and reign for the conversion of the world? How can men believe such doctrines when not one text in the Bible teaches such things? Peter refers specifically to God's dealings with Sodom and Gomorrah as a warning and ensample "unto those that after should live ungodly." Angels that sinned were cast down to hell. The antediluvian "world of the ungodly" were destroyed by the flood. The cities of Sodom and Gomorrah were destroyed by a visitation of God's wrath and vengeance. How forcible comes the language of the apostle: "Behold therefore the goodness and severity of God"; "knowing therefore the terror of the Lord, we persuade men." There are two sides to the character of God: one is love, mercy, long-suffering, and goodness; the other is justice, judgment, anger, wrath, and vengeance. Noah, a preacher of righteousness, was a recipient of God's love and mercy, but the impenitent world of the ungodly received the just measure of God's wrath and vengeance. Just so it was at the destruction of Sodom: Lot, who was a righteous man, was delivered, but at the same time God rained fire and brimstone from heaven upon the wicked inhabitants of the land. In the foregoing text Peter clearly shows that God will deal with all men after the same manner in the great day of judgment. Sinner, take warning. Instead of Christ's coming ushering in a day of mercy and salvation to the unsaved, he hath reserved "the unjust unto the day of judgment TO BE PUNISHED."

Hear this: "Therefore be ye also ready: for in such an hour as ye think

not the Son of man cometh. Who then
is a faithful and wise servant, whom his
Lord hath made ruler over his household, to give them meat in due season?
Blessed is that servant, whom his Lord
when he cometh shall find so doing.
Verily I say unto you, that he shall make
him ruler over all his goods. But and
if that evil servant shall say in his
heart, My Lord delayeth his coming;
and shall begin to smite his fellow-serv-
ants, and to eat and drink with the
drunken; the Lord of that servant shall
come in a day when he looketh not for
him, and in an hour that he is not aware
of, and shall cut him asunder, and appoint him his portion with the hypocrites: there shall be weeping and
gnashing of teeth" (Matt. 24: 44-51).
This scripture teaches that the coming
of Christ is the next great event the
church is to look for. A solemn charge
is given to be ready. The "faithful and
wise servant" who represents those who

have obtained salvation and who diligently serve God in life, walking in all
holy conversation and godliness —
"blessed is that servant, whom his Lord
when he cometh shall find so doing."
These servants will then be rewarded
in heaven. But how will the "evil servant" fare, who in life failed to obtain
salvation, but with a mere profession
lived a selfish, ungodly life? Will such
have further opportunities of salvation?
"The Lord of that servant shall come in
a day when he looketh not for him, and
in an hour that he is not aware of, and
shall cut him asunder, and appoint him
his portion with the hypocrites: there
shall be weeping and gnashing of
teeth." How different the teaching of
Millennial Dawn, which says that there
will be given to all men another and a
better chance. Reader, which will you
believe? "Let God be true." Amen.

In Matt. 25: 1-13 the kingdom of
heaven is likened unto ten virgins.

"While the bridegroom tarried, they all slumbered and slept." This refers to the general stupidity and formality that prevails. The cry, "Behold the bridegroom cometh," is the discovery and announcement of the signs of his near approach. The wise virgins are those saints who have their vessels (hearts) filled with the Holy Spirit, the Sanctifier. The foolish are all formalists and deceived professors, who know they are not saved now, but hope to be some time in the future; also, those who have been saved and afterwards failed to walk in the light of the Word. At the coming of Christ they will find their lamps are going out. In the greatest emergency their religion fails them, and their false hope expires. Oh, the millions that will meet the fate of the foolish virgins in that day! Will there then come a thousand years of mercy, offered to all of Adam's race? Nay; only "they that were READY went in with him to

the marriage: and the door was shut."
Too late! Too late! No more opportunity for all the foolish, empty-hearted
professors to get ready. They will then
begin to cry, "Lord, Lord, open to us."
Hear the answer: "I know you not."
Could language be framed to teach
more clearly that the second coming of
Christ will eternally fix the destiny of
all men? "Watch therefore; for ye
know neither the day nor the hour
wherein the Son of man cometh."

"The kingdom of heaven is as a man
traveling into a far country, who called
his own servants, and delivered unto
them his goods" (Matt. 25:14). Christ
has gone into heaven, where he is
seated at the right hand of the Father.
He has left us his salvation, love, meek-
ness, gentleness, goodness, faith, etc.,
to develop and manifest in our lives.
Great responsibilities rest upon us in exercising the talents he has given us in
doing good and laboring for the salva-

tion of men. Some are faithful, others are not. "After a long time the lord of those servants cometh, and reckoneth with them" (v. 19). This refers to Christ's coming to judgment. To the faithful, who in life improved their talents for good, he will say: "Well done, good and faithful servant: thou hast been faithful over a few things, . . . enter thou into the joy of thy Lord" (v. 23). But what about the unfaithful — will they have a second chance? No; the Lord will say to such, "Thou wicked and slothful servant." "Cast ye the unprofitable servant into outer darkness: there shall be weeping and gnashing of teeth" (vs. 26, 30).

In Rev. 11: 18 we read a description of the final judgment: "Thy wrath is come, and the time of the dead, that they should be judged, and that thou shouldest give reward unto thy servants the prophets, and to the saints, and them that fear thy name, small and

great; and shouldest destroy them
which destroy the earth." Here, again,
we read of God's wrath upon the ungodly, also of the reward of the saints,
both of which are given in the day when
the dead are judged; which, as before
proved, takes place at Christ's coming.
"When the Son of man shall come in
his glory, and all the holy angels with
him, then shall he sit upon the throne
of his glory: and before him shall be
gathered all nations: and he shall separate them one from another, as a shepherd divideth his sheep from the goats:
and he shall set the sheep [righteous]
on his right hand, but the goats
[wicked] on the left. Then shall the
King say unto them on his right hand,
Come, ye blessed of my Father, inherit
the kingdom prepared for you from the
foundation of the world. . . . Then
shall he say also unto them on the left
hand, Depart from me, ye cursed, into
everlasting fire, prepared for the devil

and his angels. . . . And these shall go away into everlasting punishment: but the righteous unto life eternal" (Matt. 25: 31-46).

Why multiply texts of scripture? Nothing is said about setting up a kingdom and reigning a thousand years for the conversion of the world. Such a belief is the result of a faith that lives outside of the Bible in the mists and fogs of ignorance and superstition. But the plain teaching of Jesus is that the final and eternal separation of the righteous and the wicked—the rewarding and receiving of the righteous into his heavenly kingdom, and the casting of the wicked into everlasting punishment—will all take place "when the Son of man shall come in his glory." Amen. Even so come, Lord Jesus.

A DAY OF WRATH

The Scriptures abundantly prove that we are now living in a day of infinite

mercy and salvation for a lost world,
and that a day of wrath and vengeance
is approaching, a time when "it will be
a fearful thing to fall into the hands
of the living God." John the Baptist
warned the people "to flee from the
WRATH TO COME" (Matt. 3:7).
"But after thy hardness and impenitent
heart treasurest up unto thyself wrath
against the day of wrath, and revelation of the righteous judgment of God;
who will render to every man according
to his deeds" (Rom. 2:5, 6).

We read of the "vials full of the
wrath of God"; of "the fierce anger of
the Lord"; of "the wine of the wrath
of God, which is poured out without
mixture into the cup of his indignation"; of "the fierceness and wrath of
Almighty God"; and of God's wrath
waxing hot. These expressions convey
to our minds what a terrible day of the
Lord is impending, which will soon

break forth upon the world of the ungodly.

"God is jealous, and the Lord revengeth; the Lord revengeth, and is furious; the Lord will take vengeance on his adversaries, and he reserveth wrath for his enemies. The Lord . . . will not at all acquit the wicked: the Lord hath his way in the whirlwind and in the storm. . . . The mountains quake at him, and the hills melt, and the earth is burned at his presence, yea, the world, and all that dwell therein. Who can stand before his indignation? and who can abide in the fierceness of his anger? His fury is poured out like fire" (Nahum 1: 2-6). "Upon the wicked he shall rain snares, fire and brimstone, and an horrible tempest: this shall be the portion of their cup" (Psa. 11: 6). "For the great day of his wrath is come; and who shall be able to stand?" (Rev. 6: 17).

A DAY OF REWARDS

The Bible does not teach that the full reward of the righteous will be given in the hour of death, but the reward is always associated with Christ's second coming. The familiar promise of Christ to his disciples relative to their future and eternal home, points to his coming as the time when they will receive it. "I go to prepare a place for you. And if I go and prepare a place for you, **I will come again,** and receive you unto myself; that where I am, there ye may be also" (John 14: 2, 3).

The above scripture harmonizes with the Lord's statement through the Revelator, "And, behold, I come quickly; and my reward is with me, to give to every man according as his work shall be" (Rev. 22: 12). Paul's last testimony regarding his future reward, was: "I am now ready to be offered, and the time of my departure is at hand. I have fought a good fight, I have finished my

AND WHAT WILL FOLLOW

course, I have kept the faith: henceforth there is laid up for me a crown of righteousness, which the Lord, the righteous judge, shall give me AT THAT DAY: and not to me only, but unto all them also that love his appearing" (2 Tim. 4: 6-8). This last text clearly proves that the apostle and all those who are saved will be crowned, not at death, but "at that day," which is defined as the day of "his appearing."

"The crowning day is coming, is coming by and by,
When our Lord shall come with power and glory
from on high,
Oh, that glorious sight will gladden each waiting,
watchful eye,
In the crowning day that's coming by and by."

"Heaven and Earth Shall Pass Away"

Both the Old and the New Testament scriptures teach that this earth will have an end, that it will finally pass out of existence. "Of old thou hast laid the foundation of the earth; and the heav-

ens are the work of thy hands. They
shall perish, but thou shalt endure"
(Psa. 102: 25, 26). "The earth is utterly broken down, the earth is clean
dissolved, the earth is moved exceedingly. The earth shall reel to and fro
like a drunkard, and shall be removed
like a cottage; . . . it shall fall, and
not rise again" (Isa. 24: 19, 20). "Lift
up your eyes to the heavens, and look
upon the earth beneath; for the heavens
shall vanish away like smoke, and the
earth shall wax old like a garment"
(Isa. 51: 6). "Till heaven and earth
pass" (Matt. 5: 18). "Heaven and
earth shall pass away" (Matt. 24: 35;
Mark 13: 31; Luke 21: 33). This planet called the earth shall "wax old" and
"shall perish." It shall be "clean dissolved," "shall pass away," "and shall
be removed like a cottage"; "it shall fall
and not rise again." So positively
teaches the Word of God.

Now, when will the passing away of

this earth take place? Answer. "And I saw a great white throne, and him that sat on it, from whose face the earth and the heaven fled away; and there was found no place for them. And I saw the dead, small and great, stand before God. . . . and the dead were judged," etc. (Rev. 20: 11, 12). The coming of Christ upon the great white throne—"the throne of his glory" (Matt. 25: 31)—the coming forth of all the dead from land and sea, the time of the judgment, will be the time when this earth will pass away and no place be found for it. Let all our readers prepare for such a catastrophe; for as truly as God has spoken, it will come. The "heavens" in these texts refers to the aerial heavens. (For comments read Gen. 7: 3, 23; Jer. 9: 10; 10: 13; 14: 22; Zech. 8: 12.)

We shall next notice the manner in which it will pass away. "But the heavens and the earth which are now,

by the same word are kept in store, reserved unto fire against the day of
judgment and perdition of ungodly
men. But, beloved, be not ignorant of
this one thing, that one day is with the
Lord as a thousand years, and a thousand years as one day. The Lord is
not slack concerning his promise, as
some men count slackness; but is long-
suffering to us-ward, not willing that
any should perish, but that all should
come to repentance. But the day of the
Lord will come as a thief in the night;
in the which the heavens shall pass
away with a great noise, and the elements shall melt with fervent heat, the
earth also and the works that are therein shall be burned up. Seeing then that
all these things shall be dissolved, what
manner of persons ought ye to be in all
holy conversation and godliness, looking for and hasting unto the coming of
the day of God, wherein the heavens
being on fire shall be dissolved, and the

elements shall melt with fervent heat? . . . Wherefore, beloved, seeing that ye look for such things, be diligent that ye may be found of him in peace, without spot, and blameless. And account that the long-suffering of our Lord is salvation" (2 Pet. 3: 7-15). How clear this testimony! Not only will the works in this earth be consumed, but the earth itself "shall be burned up," "dissolved," and "melted with fervent heat." That day of fire which shall consume this earth, "the day of judgment and perdition of ungodly men," will be the day of the Lord's second advent (see vs. 4, 10). We will here insert an able exposition of this scripture, from the pen of Brother D. S. Warner.

"Instead of conveying an idea that this last destruction will only be similar to that of the flood, a contrast is drawn between the two. The first was only by water; the next shall be by fire, and surely God knew that we understood

the difference between the action of
these two elements. Floods of water
may carry away buildings, and wreck
them, and wash the earth over cities,
etc.; but they have no power to take
out of existence a single stone or piece
of timber. Whereas fire actually consumes, and changes things from a visible existence into a small bit of ashes
and vapor, and reduces even earth and
stone back to a melted mass, as it was
before the completion of creation work;
and we are plainly told that this very
destruction will come to pass. Again,
observe the contrasted extent of the two
destructions. 'The world that then was,
being overflowed with water perished.'
But the next time both the heavens and
the earth shall be dissolved. So we see
clearly that the 'end of all things' does
not mean a renovation of this earth; but
an utter consuming, and melting of the
same into the same chaotic state in

which its matter existed before the completion of creation.

"Again, right in the seventh verse we have a positive overthrow of the whole millennial theory. They tell us that this destruction by fire will only renovate the earth, and that then there will be an earthly reign of one thousand years, after which will come the resurrection and the judgment of the wicked. But the fire which millenarians locate before the thousand years, the Word identifies with the 'judgment and perdition of the ungodly,' an event which they say will take place after the thousand years. Do you see the point? The very thing which they think will prepare the earth for their fancied millennium, God associates with that which they say will come after the millennium. So they are mistaken, or the Word of God is wrong. But the word of the Lord is right, and every contrary doctrine is false. Behold the harmony of divine truth!

"The Scriptures very clearly teach
that Christ will come in the end of the
world, in the last day of this last age
of time. The Scriptures also inform us
that this last day will be the day of
judgment. And here Peter tells us
plainly that on that very day of his coming and the judgment, the heavens and
the earth will be consumed, melted, and
destroyed. So this time will indeed be
the end of the world, the close of all
time allotted to this earth. On the eighth
verse theological speculators have taken
the authority to say that the earth will
stand in its present condition just six
thousand years, and the seventh thousand will be a millennial rest. But no
such thought is found in the text or context. 'One day is with the Lord as a
thousand years, and a thousand years
as one day.' The expression is used
simply to assure us that the promises of
God do not become doubtful because of
long delay; that the word of God that

is deferred two thousand years is just as sure as that which is fulfilled in the same week or month it was spoken. Just so the apostle Peter applies his words in the next verse, saying, 'The Lord is not slack concerning his promises, as some men count slackness.' How do men count slackness? When men make promises, leaving the time indefinite, it is natural for us to lose confidence in proportion to the delay. Men actually count others slack in their word, if long deferred. But God is not slack in his promises, as men count their fellow men slack; nay, in this respect, a thousand years is with the Lord as one day. In other words, his promise is just as sure to come to pass though deferred ten thousand years, as if it were fulfilled in ten days. For two reasons this is so: he says, 'I am the Lord, I change not'; and 'I will remember my covenant.' He never forgets the words he has spoken.

"In this chapter the coming of Christ,

the day of judgment, and the utter destruction of the earth and its works are
all pointed forward to as the events of
one great and last 'day of God, wherein the heavens [the atmosphere] being
on fire shall be dissolved, and the elements [that compose the earth] shall
melt with fervent heat' (v. 12).

"Now let us see if any offers of salvation to our race will extend beyond
that awful day.   Owing to the long
pending of Christ's second advent, it
was foreseen that 'there shall come in
the last days scoffers, walking after
their own lusts, and saying, Where is
the promise of his coming?' Wherefore the Lord, by this inspired writer,
explains the reason of his delay. 'The
Lord is not slack concerning his promise, as some men count slackness; but
is long-suffering to us-ward, not willing
that any should perish, but that all
should come to repentance' (v. 9). 'And

account that the long-suffering of our Lord is salvation' (v. 15).

"Surely this is all very plain. The long pending of Christ's second advent, we are told, is not because of any slackness on the part of the Lord to fulfil his promise, but because he is not willing that poor sinners should be cut off from all hope, and eternally perish. We are, therefore, taught to count that the long-suffering, the prolonged delay of the Lord and the day of judgment, 'is salvation'—that men may have extended time for repentance and salvation.

"So let all men take warning that 'salvation' is now, and only now, is all on this side the coming of the Lord; whereas his second coming will be the 'day of judgment and perdition of ungodly men,' the point at which all salvation-work will be forever cut off. Is it not one of the most astonishing things that have ever been invented, that men

—such, for instance, as C. T. Russell, the age-to-come teacher—can be so subverted as to teach that now is not the time of salvation, but that that glorious work is 'deferred until after Christ's second advent, in the millennial age'? How dare men teach such shocking falsehoods in the face of God's Word? Truth declares that now is the day of salvation, and that the present day of grace is drawn out by the mercy of God, to enable more lost sinners to be saved; and that when Christ comes salvation will forever cease, the judgment and perdition of all the wicked take place, and this earth perish. 'But the day of the Lord will come as a thief in the night; in the which the heavens shall pass away with a great noise, and the elements shall melt with fervent heat, the earth also and the works that are therein shall be burned up' (v. 10). This is so plain that comment is scarcely needed.

"Christ told his church that he would come at a time when not looked for. Peter's words here convey the same idea. And in that day of the Lord's coming 'the heavens [the aerial heavens] will pass away with a great noise, and the elements shall melt; the earth and the works therein shall be burned up.' The atmosphere, earth, and all in it, even all the elements that compose this globe shall be melted and burned up. In verse eleven it is again repeated that 'all these things shall be dissolved,' and we are solemnly charged in view of this coming crisis to live 'in all holy conversation and godliness, looking for and hasting unto the coming of the day of God, wherein the heavens being on fire shall be dissolved, and the elements [of this earth] shall melt with fervent heat.' These scriptures, it would seem, can not be misconstrued. They emphatically teach us that the earth and all pertaining to it, at the coming of

Christ and the day of judgment, will be reduced back to a melted and chaotic state, without form and void, as its matter existed before the completion of creation. 'Wherefore, beloved, seeing that ye look for such things, be diligent that ye may be found of him in peace, without spot and blameless.'

"Oh, that vain speculators upon the solemn subjects of prophecy, and all their deceived readers, would stop and consider the loud warnings from the Almighty everywhere associated with the second advent of Christ! Instead of ushering in an age of restitution of souls from sin, and millennial glory, it will consign to eternal despair all who will not be found in peace, 'without spot and blameless.' Reader, is that your happy condition just now? If not, rest not until the blood of Christ is applied, which 'cleanseth from all sin.' All these scriptures teach that we are living in the last dispensation of time; that 'now is

the day of salvation'; that at the second
advent of Christ he will not set up a
kingdom, but will deliver up the kingdom to the Father, and close his personal reign (1 Cor. 10:23, 24); that at
his coming all the dead will be raised,
all men judged, the righteous crowned
in heaven and the wicked sentenced to
'everlasting punishment,' this earth, and
all the works that are in it burned up,
and pass away, and time and probation end.

"Christ's second advent is urged upon
the church in the present age as a strong
inducement to watch and pray, to live
holy, and be ready for the same, with
the solemn warning that our eternal
destiny, of either reward or punishment, will depend upon the condition
we shall be found in at that instant.
Therefore the coming described is not
one that will be pending in a future
age, but the crisis that shall close the
present age. Otherwise it would not

have been charged upon this age to
keep it in view. He that is unjust, filthy,
or righteous and holy, let him be so
still, is directly connected with 'Behold,
I come quickly and my reward is with
me to give to every man [both saint and
sinner] according as his work shall be.'
The coincidence of the coming of
Christ and the general judgment is utterly fatal to the millennial theory. And
now we have proved that at the time of
his revelation from heaven with power
and great glory, the earth will be
burned up, and pass away, leaving no
possible place for the millennial dream
to be enacted. Are you ready for that
great day? If not, 'today, if ye will
hear his voice, harden not your hearts.'
'Behold, now is the day of salvation,'
'and after this the judgment.' Amen."

Hell the Eternal Abode of the Ungodly

With respect to the eternal destiny of mankind, the Bible teaches but two places of abode; namely, **heaven** and **hell;** the former to be the abode of the righteous, the latter of the wicked. In these days of skepticism and unbelief the Bible doctrine of hell has become very unpopular. Indeed, I think I am safe in saying that not one half of the Protestant ministry believe it, and that a much less number teach it. The tendency of the times is to seek some doctrine that will lessen the fears of hell and soothe the sinner and the cold, "twice dead" professor of Christianity on the road to perdition. A radical preacher like John the Baptist or Jesus Christ himself, who warned men of the impending "damnation of hell" and "wrath to come," is not popular with the masses. Such teaching, it is claimed, is far behind the times. But what says

the Bible? This is the book to which
we appeal as the standard of decision
on all such questions. The Scripture
can not be broken. Eternal truth will
stand when all the doctrines and theories of men have passed away.

THERE IS A HELL INTO WHICH THE WICKED
WILL BE CAST

"The wicked shall be turned into
hell" (Psa. 9: 17). "Shall be in danger
of **hell fire**" (Matt. 5: 22). "Thy whole
body should be cast into **hell**" (Matt.
5: 29, 30). "Both soul and body in
hell" (Matt. 10: 28). "Cast into **hell
fire**" (Matt. 18: 9). "Child of **hell**"
(Matt. 23: 15). "How can ye escape
the damnation of **hell**?" (Matt. 23: 33).
"To go into **hell**" (Mark 9: 43). "Cast
into **hell**" (Mark 9: 45, 47). "Set on
fire of **hell**" (Jas. 3: 6). "Cast them
down to **hell**" (2 Pet. 2: 4). Thus we
could multiply texts on this important
point. But let it be remembered that

one clear text is as good as a thousand, for truth never crosses itself, truth never contradicts. Is it not a marvel that in the face of such a solid bulwark of eternal truth men will deny that there is a hell? As well deny that there is a God and a heaven in which he dwells.

"But," says the disputer, "**hell** means the grave and the valley of Hinnom." So saying, he lights on the original words—**Sheol, Hades, Tartaros,** and **Gehenna**—and tries to place such construction on these terms as will explain away the solemn warnings of Christ and the apostles, namely, that wicked men will suffer an awful punishment in hell-fire forever. I have never met an advocate of false doctrine but would delve into Greek terms and try to explain away the clear statements of Scripture by his peculiar interpretation of the original. There may be a few Scripture texts where the word translated "hell" is used out of its regular order and applied to the grave. But "Sheol" and its counterpart "Hades" properly apply to the state and abode of the soul after death. "Burn unto the lowest hell" (Deut. 32: 22). "The wicked shall be turned into hell [Sheol], and all the nations that forget God" (Psa. 9: 17). "In hell [Hades] he lift up his eyes, being in torments." "I am tormented in this flame" (Luke 16: 23, 24). To say this refers to the grave is ridiculous.

The lowest Hades is a place of torment. The fire of Gehenna is that into which the wicked will be cast in the great day of judgment and be tormented, "where their worm dieth not." So, whether we have the word "Hades," denoting the state of the wicked between death and the judgment, or "Gehenna," their abode beyond the judgment, it will be hell in tormenting flame.

HELL WILL BE A PLACE OF FIRE

"It is better for thee to enter into life with one eye, rather than having two eyes to be cast into **hell fire**" (Matt. 18: 9). "And whosoever was not found written in the book of life was cast into the **lake of fire**" (Rev. 20: 15). False religionists will "go into perdition," to **"the burning flame"** (Rev. 17: 8; Dan. 7: 11). "These both were cast alive into a **lake of fire burning with brimstone"** (Rev. 19: 20). "But the fearful, and unbelieving, and the abominable, and murderers, and whoremongers, and sorcerers, and idolators, and all liars, shall have their part in the **lake which burneth with fire and brimstone**; which is the second death" (Rev. 21: 8). "The same shall drink of the wine of the wrath of God, which is poured out without mixture into the cup of his indignation; and he shall be **tormented with fire and brimstone** . . . and the smoke of their torment ascendeth up forever and ever: and they have no rest day nor night" (Rev. 14: 10, 11). "And shall cast them into a **furnace of fire:** there shall be wailing and gnashing of teeth" (Matt. 13: 42). "So shall it be at the end of the world: the angels shall come forth, and sever the wicked from among the just, and shall cast them into the **furnace of fire:** there shall be wailing and gnashing of teeth" (Matt. 13: 49, 50). "Then the Lord rained upon Sodom and upon Gomorrah **brimstone and fire from the Lord** out of heaven" (Gen. 19: 24).

"But the same day that Lot went out of Sodom **it rained fire and brimstone from heaven,** and destroyed them all. **Even thus shall it be in the day when the Son of man is revealed**" (Luke 17: 29, 30). "Upon the wicked he shall rain snares, fire and brimstone, and an horrible tempest: this shall be the portion of their cup" (Psa. 11: 6). "And fire came down from God out of heaven, and devoured them" (Rev. 20:9). "In flaming fire taking vengeance on them that know not God" (2 Thess. 1:8). "And the devil that deceived them was cast into the lake of fire and brimstone" (Rev. 20:10).

Surely these fourteen texts of scripture are conclusive on this subject. They declare that when Christ shall be revealed from heaven, he will come in flaming fire, and will rain upon the wicked fire and brimstone from heaven; that the wicked will then be cast into "hell-fire," which is termed "a furnace of fire," a "lake of fire and brimstone." In this awful place of fire they will "wail and gnash their teeth." It matters not whether this fire is literal or symbolic. However, I do not believe that, as Adventists teach, the fire of hell will be the same as the fire that consumes brush or stubble. It seems probable that literal fire could not affect spiritual beings. But whether literal or symbolic, it will be punishment—a punishment so terrible that it is fitly represented to us as **fire.**

"And in hell he lift up his eyes, being in torments, and seeth Abraham afar off, and Lazarus in his bosom. And he cried and said, Father Abraham, have mercy on me, and send Lazarus, that he may dip the tip of his finger in water, and cool my tongue; for I am tormented in this flame" (Luke 16: 23, 24). This poor man remembered that on earth water would quench fire and thirst and would cool a parched tongue. His flames of torment were such that he naturally craved water. He cried for mercy and begged for water; but there is no water in hell. The ultimate state of the wicked will be in a place termed a "furnace of fire," "lake of fire burning with brimstone." "flames of torment." So teaches the Bible; and "who art thou that repliest against God?"

THE FIRES OF HELL WILL BURN FOREVER

We have seen that the Scriptures clearly teach that the wicked in the great day of judgment will be cast into hell, into a "lake of fire and brimstone," termed "hell-fire." But how long will the fires of hell burn? "Then shall he say unto them on the left hand, Depart from me, ye cursed, into **everlasting** fire, prepared for the devil and his angels" (Matt. 25: 41). "Cast into **everlasting** fire" (Matt. 18: 8). "Suffering the vengeance of **eternal** fire" (Jude 7). "And if thy hand offend thee, cut it off: it is better for thee to enter into life maimed, than having two hands to go **into hell**, into the fire that **never shall be quenched**: where their worm dieth not, and the fire **is not quenched**. And if thy foot offend thee, cut it off: it is better for thee to enter halt into life, than having two feet to be cast into hell, into the fire that **never shall be quenched**:

where their worm dieth not, and the
fire is **not quenched**. And if thine eye
offend thee, pluck it out: it is better for
thee to enter into the kingdom of God
with one eye, than having two eyes to
be cast into **hell-fire**: where their worm
dieth not, and the fire is **not quenched**"
(Mark 9: 43-48). "And these shall go
away into **everlasting** punishment"
(Matt. 25: 46).

In plain, unmistakable language the
terrible doom of the guilty is here foretold. Whether men believe it or not,
some day they will awaken to its awful
realization. Some day they will fully
comprehend the eternal loss of their
priceless souls. The many scriptures I
have cited teach that the wicked will be
cast into an everlasting hell and will
there suffer everlasting punishment.
Sixteen positive texts of Scripture declare that the wicked will be turned into
"hell," termed "hell-fire," "furnace of
fire," "lake of fire and brimstone"; that

this fire will be an "everlasting fire," a fire that "never shall be quenched"; and that in this fire the wicked will "wail and gnash their teeth" and will suffer an "everlasting punishment." If they suffer an "everlasting punishment," there will be no end to that punishment. The everlasting fires of hell in which they will suffer this punishment never will be quenched; hence they will burn forever.

These expressions, some say, are only figures of the sinner's doom. If so, there would be no room to ease the guilty conscience. For if such expressions as those I have quoted are only figures of future punishment, I ask in Jesus' name, What must the reality be? All must admit that the reality is greater than the figure. If all the expressions in the texts cited above are but figures of future punishment, then the reality will be far greater.

THE PUNISHMENT OF THE GUILTY WILL BE UNENDING

In the twenty-fifth chapter of Matthew is recorded a description of the final judgment, in Christ's own words. Surely what he said will stand. Who dare reply against Him whose sayings can not be broken, and whose words are the truth? He clearly tells us what the ultimate destiny of both righteous and wicked will be. A final separation will be made. To those on his right hand he will say, "Come, ye blessed of my Father, inherit the kingdom" and, "Well done, good and faithful servant; . . . enter thou into the joy of thy lord" (v. 23). To those on the left hand he will say, "Depart from me, ye cursed, into everlasting fire, prepared for the devil and his angels" (v. 41). "Cast ye the unprofitable servant into outer darkness: there shall be weeping and gnashing of teeth" (v. 30). "And these shall go away into everlasting punishment:

but the righteous into life eternal" (v. 46).

Facts and truths are stubborn things Indeed, truth can never be destroyed. In unmistakable plainness Jesus tells us just what the doom of the sinner will be beyond the judgment. Note the contrast between the destiny of the righteous and that of the wicked: "Come, ye blessed"; "Depart, ye cursed." The former will enter "into the joy of the Lord"; the latter will "go away" into "outer darkness," "everlasting fire," where there will be "weeping and gnashing of teeth." What an awful sentence—"Depart"! This means the punishment of loss, or privation. "Ye can not, ye shall not, be united to me—depart from me." Oh, terrible word! and yet a worse to come—**"into everlasting fire."** This is the punishment of sense. "Ye shall not only be separated from me, but be tormented—awfully, everlastingly tormented in that place of separation." In Mark 9: 43-48 Jesus Christ three times over declares that the wicked shall go into hell, into "the fire that never shall be quenched: . . . where their worm dieth not, and the fire is not quenched." If hell-fire will never be quenched, it will burn forever; and so positively teaches the Bible—"Cast into **everlasting fire**" (Matt. 18: 8). There shall be wailing and gnashing of teeth "where their worm dieth not." Mark you, every one has his own worm —"**their** worm."

The guilty conscience of man will live forever and torment the wicked while eternity's cycles roll. "These shall go away into **everlasting** punishment"— no appeal, no remedy, to all eternity! There will be no end to the punishment of those whose final impenitence manifests in them an eternal will and desire to sin. By dying in opposition to God, they cast themselves necessarily into a state of continual separation from him.

How, then, can this punishment have an end? Will the glory and joy of the righteous ever end? Jesus uses the same word (aionios) to express and measure the duration of future punishment that is used to express the duration of the state of glory. The original word means "indeterminate as to duration," "everlasting," "perpetual." The righteous, called "blessed," will enter life eternal (aionios). The wicked, called "cursed," will depart and go away into everlasting (aionios) fire, and will there suffer an everlasting (aionios) punishment. Jesus himself said so. They are not annihilated, but they go into fire and remain there in punishment. How long? As long as the righteous live—eternally.

It is utterly absurd to say that a man still suffers after he has been annihilated. That which ceases to be, ceases to suffer. Can a pile of ashes suffer? Can a being reduced to nonentity weep,

wail, and gnash teeth? Such teaching
betrays ignorance and blindness. Is
"everlasting punishment" in "everlasting fire" annihilation? "He lift up his
eyes being in torments"; he cried, "I am
tormented in this flame," "this place of
torment" (Luke 16). Could an annihilated being "lift up his eyes" or cry?
No indeed. If souls go into punishment,
they must continue to exist; for ashes
can not be punished.

Hell was "prepared for the devil and
his angels" (Matt. 25: 41). It was not
designed for human souls. "But as the
wicked are partakers with the devil and
his angels in their iniquities, in their
rebellion against God; so it is right that
they should be sharers with them in
their punishment. We see plainly why
sinners will be so punished; not because
there was no salvation for them, but
because they neglected to receive good
and do good. As they received not the
Christ who was offered to them, they

could not do the work of righteousness which was required of them. They are cursed, because they refused to be blessed; they are damned, because they refused to be saved."

The word "everlasting" measures both the fire of hell and the punishment of the wicked therein. I shall cite a few texts to give its use in the Old Testament: "The everlasting God" (Gen. 21: 33), "thy kingdom [God's kingdom] is an everlasting kingdom" (Psa. 145: 13), "the everlasting Father" (Isa. 9: 6), "everlasting joy" (Isa. 35: 10), "everlasting salvation" (Isa. 45: 17), God is "an everlasting king" (Jer. 10: 10), God's love is "an everlasting love" (Jer. 31: 3), God will have "everlasting dominion" (Dan. 7: 14), Messiah was to bring "everlasting righteousness" (Dan. 9: 24), and the wicked will suffer "SHAME AND EVERLASTING CONTEMPT" (Dan. 12: 2). Therefore as long as God himself shall exist, and as long as he shall have dominion, the wicked will "suffer shame and everlasting contempt." The same word that measures the endless existence of God himself, of his kingdom, dominion, salvation, love, joy, and righteousness, measures the shame and contempt of the wicked. How dare men, in the face of this solemn and awful truth, teach that it will come to an end? The word "everlasting" means to all eternity.

Let us notice the New Testament use of the word: "everlasting life" (Rom. 6: 22), "everlasting gospel" (Rev. 14: 6), "everlasting kingdom" (2 Pet. 1: 11), "everlasting God" (Rom. 16: 26), "these shall go away into everlasting punishment" (Matt. 25: 46); "Depart from me, ye cursed, into everlasting fire prepared for the devil and his angels" (Matt. 25: 41). Note that the same word that measures the life of the righteous, that measures the existence of the gospel, that measures the duration of

God's kingdom and the existence of God himself, measures the punishment of the wicked in hell-fire. If the everlasting God will continue to exist throughout endless ages, then the wicked will suffer throughout endless ages. To deny this is to make the truth a lie; and every honest soul cries out, "Nay, let God be true, though every man be a liar."

In 2 Thess. 1: 9 it is clearly stated that the awful glory of God at his coming will drive the wicked from his presence into "everlasting" destruction. None can stand before him but those who in life live on the plane of his nature and possess his holiness. How, then, can any soul with the smallest spot of sin hope to stand before God in the awful day of his coming and judgment? How many plain and solemn warnings God has given to all men, of that day when all must either stand or fall in the presence of his majesty and glory! Hell and the lake of fire and brimstone are the same. It will be the final, the eternal place of the impenitent. "Upon it falls the curtain of everlasting night! No voice echoes back its horrors. No light gleams from its lurid burnings. No revolution of cycles numbers the measure of its years. Eternity, dark, fathomless, hopeless, seals the fate of all adjudged to dwell amid the devouring fires, amid everlasting burnings."

In Psa. 9: 17 it is stated that "the wicked shall be turned into **hell,** and all the nations that forget God." Here the psalmist is certainly speaking of the ultimate state of the ungodly. Some, however, may say that the original word is "Sheol." Yes; "hell" in every Old Testament text is from either "Sheol" (Hebrew) or its counterpart, "Hades" (Greek). The word "Gehenna" is nowhere found in the Old Testament. In the New Testament, however, Gehenna is used to denote the place of eternal punishment beyond the resurrection.

The lowest Hades is a place of fire and torment. "Shall burn unto the lowest hell [Sheol or Hades]" (Deut. 32: 22). "In hell [Hades] he lift up his eyes, being in torments," and cried, "I am tormented in this flame," "this place of torment" (Luke 16). Since to the souls of wicked men Sheol is a place of fire and torment, the psalmist uses the same word to denote the place of final and eternal punishment. David is certainly speaking of what will take place at the judgment. The wicked (all the ungodly) and the nations that forget God (those nations who retained not God in their knowledge); in fact, all the unsaved, will be **turned into hell.** The original signifies "cast into," "driven away into." David speaks of a time when all the wicked together will be driven away into fire and torment. He refers to the final and awful doom

of the ungodly—to the doom of the
wicked exclusively.

HELL WILL BE A PLACE OF DARKNESS— NIGHT

"I say unto you, That many shall
come from the east and west, and shall
sit down with Abraham, and Isaac, and
Jacob, in the kingdom of heaven. But
the children of the kingdom shall be
cast out into outer darkness: there shall
be weeping and gnashing of teeth"
(Matt. 8: 11, 12). "Cast ye the unprofitable servant into outer darkness:
there shall be weeping and gnashing of
teeth" (Matt. 25: 30). "Bind him hand
and foot, and take him away, and cast
him into outer darkness; there shall be
weeping and gnashing of teeth" (Matt.
22: 13). "And shall cut him asunder,
and appoint him his portion with the
hypocrites: there shall be weeping and
gnashing of teeth" (Matt. 24: 51).
"And shall cast them into a furnace of

fire: there shall be wailing and gnashing of teeth" (Matt. 13:42).

How solemn and awful these truths!
Now is the day of salvation, the accepted time to seek God; but the time is
coming when mercy's door will forever
close. Now the world's Redeemer and
Savior mediates in behalf of lost hu-
manity; but the time is coming when he
will leave the mediatorial throne for the
judgment-seat. Then the world will be
without an advocate, without a Savior,
or further opportunity of salvation. The
wrath of God will be poured out on his
enemies. The unprofitable servant, the
false prophet, the deceived millions,
with all the host of apostates and blasphemers that have despised Christ's
name and trampled on his blood, will
then be "cast out" into "outer darkness." There they "will have their portion with the hypocrites," where there
shall be "weeping and gnashing of
teeth."

This is directly opposite to annihilation. "Hell," "furnace of fire," and "outer darkness" all express punishment. "Bind him hand and foot, and take him away." Oh, awful doom! the punishment of separation—the same as that referred to in Matt. 25: 41, 46. Could this be said of ashes? But listen to the next sentence, more awful still: "And cast him into outer darkness"—night, eternity's night. Lost amid that awful darkness! "There shall be weeping and wailing and gnashing of teeth."

Does that sound like being blotted out of existence? But how long will the wicked thus suffer? How long will they remain in that awful darkness? Answer: "They shall **never** see light" (Psa. 49: 19). What awful truth! Yet, as sure as God's Word declares it, the same will come to pass. Reader, note carefully these solemn declarations of truth, which can not be broken. Those who know not God, the wicked, will be cast into "outer darkness," and in that place "they shall never see light." In that place of torment, "upon the wicked He shall rain snares, fire and brimstone, and an horrible tempest: this shall be the portion of their cup" (Psa. 11: 6). They will "weep and gnash their teeth."

Could language be framed to picture more clearly the fearful and awful doom of the ungodly? This is just the opposite of annihilation. They go into a place of punishment and remain there. They suffer there. No ray of light will ever penetrate that awful darkness. No sunbeam of hope will ever gladden their hearts—**"outer darkness."** Think of a place so far away that not a ray of light from any planet in the vast universe can reach it. Those who inhabit that dungeon of darkness, those caverns of night, "shall **never see light**," no, never.

"These are wells without water,

clouds that are carried with a tempest; to whom the mist of darkness is reserved forever" (2 Pet. 2: 17). "Raging waves of the sea, foaming out their own shame; wandering stars, to whom is reserved the blackness of darkness forever" (Jude 13). Here is pictured, by the unerring pen of inspiration, the eternity of lost souls. Immortal souls lost—lost in eternity's night; lost amid howling demons and the piercing shrieks of damned souls; lost upon the rocking billows of eternal despair; hopelessly, totally, forever lost. Clouds carried by the tempest; raging waves, foaming out their own shame; wandering stars, weeping, wailing, in the "mist of darkness"—"outer darkness"—"the blackness of darkness forever."

The word "forever" measures the length of time that the wicked will wail in the blackness of eternal night. **"FOREVER,** through eternity; through endless ages."—**Webster.** "Unlimited duration; eternity."—**Greenfield.** These definitions express the New Testament use of the word. In every New Testament text where it is found, it measures eternity. For the reader's benefit I shall here give the use of the word "forever" in the New Testament.

"And he shall reign over the house of Jacob **forever;** and of his kingdom there **shall be no end**" (Luke 1: 33). Here it is plain that "forever" is without end. "The Son abideth **forever**" (John 8: 35). "Thine is the kingdom, and the power, and the glory, **forever**" (Matt. 6: 13). "The Creator, who is blessed **forever**" (Rom. 1: 25). "To whom be glory **forever**" (Rom. 11: 36). "Jesus Christ the same yesterday, and today, and **forever**" (Heb. 13: 8). "The word of God, which liveth and abideth **forever** . . . the word of the Lord endureth **forever**" (1 Pet. 1: 23-25). "These are wells without water, clouds that are carried with a tempest; to whom the

mist of darkness is reserved **forever**"
(2 Pet. 2: 17). The wicked are "raging
waves of the sea, foaming out their own
shame; wandering stars, to whom is reserved the blackness of darkness **forever**" (Jude 13).

What a chain of heavenly truth these
texts present! The same word that
measures the reign of Christ, the glory
and dominion of the Father, the un-
changeableness of Christ, the endurance of the word of truth, and the existence of the Son of God, measures the
torments of the wicked in "the blackness of darkness forever." If "outer
darkness" shall cease to be the everlasting portion of the wicked, then Christ,
his reign, glory, dominion, and truth,
will forever cease to be; for as long as
these shall continue, outer darkness
shall continue. Forever in "outer darkness," eternity's night, drifting away
from heaven, home, loved ones; from
Jesus and all that is lovely and pure.

AND WHAT WILL FOLLOW

Night—so dark that no ray of light from heaven can ever penetrate. Awful doom!

"And he said unto them, Go ye into all the world, and preach the gospel to every creature. He that believeth and is baptized shall be saved; but he that believeth not shall be damned" (Mark 16: 15, 16). In John 3: 18 we read that such as do not believe are condemned already, and that all who now believe are already saved from their sins. Thus, accepting the gospel brings a present salvation, and rejecting it brings men under condemnation. But for all who obtain a present deliverance from sin there will be a future salvation from the wrath of God. Also, the text quoted from Mark teaches a future damnation of the wicked. Not only are they **now** condemned, but they **"shall** be damned" —future tense. Where will this damnation be fully realized? Answer: "Ye serpents, ye generation of vipers, how

can ye escape the **damnation of hell?**"
(Matt. 23 : 33). Hell is the place where
the wicked will suffer future damnation.
Their punishment is termed "the damnation of hell." But when will they suffer this punishment? "Marvel not at
this: for the hour is coming, in the
which all that are in the graves shall
hear his voice, and shall come forth;
they that have done good, unto the resurrection of life; and they that have
done evil, unto the resurrection of
damnation" (John 5 : 28, 29). The
damnation of the wicked in hell lies
beyond the final resurrection. Their
resurrection is termed "the resurrection
of damnation."

"Woe unto you, scribes and Pharisees,
hypocrites! for ye devour widows'
houses, and for a pretense make long
prayer: therefore ye shall receive the
greater damnation" (Matt. 23 : 14).
"And he said unto them in his doctrine,
Beware of the scribes which love to go

in long clothing, and love salutations
in the market-places, and the chief seats
in the synagogues, and the uppermost
rooms at feasts: which devour widows'
houses, and for a pretense make long
prayers: these shall receive greater
damnation" (Mark 12: 38-40). "Whose
judgment now of a long time lingereth
not, and their damnation slumbereth
not" (2 Pet. 2: 3). "Wherefore I say
unto you, All manner of sin and blasphemy shall be forgiven unto men: but
the blasphemy against the Holy Ghost
shall not be forgiven unto men. And
whosoever speaketh a word against the
Son of man, it shall be forgiven him:
but whosoever speaketh against the
Holy Ghost, it shall not be forgiven him,
neither in this world, neither in the
world to come" (Matt. 12: 31, 32). "But
he that shall blaspheme against the
Holy Ghost hath never forgiveness, but
is in danger of **eternal damnation**"
(Mark 3: 29).

God help you to take warning. Never allow false teachers to hide the truth from your eyes. The damnation of hell will be eternal. God's Word declares it. Christ said, "It shall not be forgiven him, neither in this world, neither in the world to come"; and that he who sins against the Holy Ghost "hath **never** forgiveness." In the flames of hell he must suffer eternal damnation. Is that annihilation? Is it a handful of ashes that "hath never forgiveness"? Will a bit of mere ashes, something without consciousness, suffer a "greater condemnation"? Absurd! "How can ye escape the damnation of hell," which is "eternal damnation"?

The continuance of the damnation of the wicked in the flames of hell is measured by the word "eternal." I shall here give the Bible use of the word: "life eternal" (Matt. 25: 46), "eternal salvation" (Heb. 5: 9), "eternal redemption" (Heb. 9: 12), "eternal

Spirit" (Heb. 9: 14), "eternal inheritance" (Heb. 9: 15), "eternal glory" (2 Tim. 2: 10), "King eternal" (1 Tim. 1: 17), "eternal God" (Deut. 33: 27), "eternal damnation" (Mark 3: 29), "suffering the vengeance of eternal fire" (Jude 7).

No earthly wisdom can overthrow these solid truths. The same word that measures the life, salvation, redemption, and inheritance of the righteous in heaven, the existence of the Spirit, yea, the existence of God himself and of his glory, measures the damnation of the wicked in hell, where they will suffer the "vengeance of eternal fire." As long as the heavens shall stand, as long as the righteous shall enjoy life, as long as glory shall last, as long as God shall exist, so long shall the punishment of the wicked last. There is no way under heaven to evade the plain testimony of the Bible on this point. Eternal truth teaches eternal damnation in eternal

fire. "He that believeth on the Son
hath everlasting life: and he that believeth not the Son shall not see life;
but the wrath of God ABIDETH ON
HIM" (John 3: 36).

That torment, and not annihilation,
will be the portion of the wicked beyond
death and the judgment, the Bible most
clearly teaches. In Hades the rich man
was in torment after death. "He lift up
his eyes, being in torments." He cried
for mercy, begged for water, and said,
"I am tormented in this flame." He
called his abode, "this place of torment." Does that sound like annihilation? Was this the moldering corpse
that was buried? It was the state and
condition of a man whose body had
been buried here on earth, but whose
spirit still lived. Souls of wicked men
dwell in torments between death and
the judgment; and in that great day of
final reckoning the devil and all his fol-

lowers will go away into everlasting fire, into Gehenna—hell.

What awaits demons in that great future? Here is the answer: Devils said to Jesus, "Art thou come hither to **torment us before the time?"** (Matt. 8: 28, 29). This is why devils believe and tremble; they know the doom that awaits them beyond the judgment-day. Did they say, "Do not annihilate us, Jesus"? Ah, no; but, "I adjure thee by God, that thou **torment** me not" (Mark 5: 7), "Art thou come hither to **torment us before the time?"** A **time** of torment is coming for Satan and all his demons. That torment will be in hell, for hell was prepared for the devil and his angels (Matt. 25: 41). Yet the ungodly will be cast into the same hell of torment. "Depart from me, ye cursed, into everlasting fire, prepared for the devil and his angels." Torment awaits the guilty.

How long will the torments of hell

last? "The same shall drink of the wine of the wrath of God, which is poured out without mixture into the cup of his indignation; and he shall be tormented with fire and brimstone. . . . And the smoke of their torment ascendeth up **forever and ever:** and they have no rest day nor night" (Rev. 14: 10, 11). This torment in a lake of fire and brimstone will continue unceasingly forever and ever.

Reader, is that annihilation? Far from it. "And the devil that deceived them was cast into the lake of fire and brimstone, . . . and shall be tormented day and night forever and ever" (Rev. 20: 10). Could an unconscious being, reduced to nonentity, be tormented forever? The scriptures we have quoted teach plainly that the wicked will be tormented in hell, with demons, forever and ever.

"Forever and ever" measures the torments of the guilty in hell. I shall give other uses of the term in the Bible: "The Lord shall reign **forever and ever**" (Exod. 15: 18). "The saints of the Most High shall take the kingdom, and possess the kingdom forever, even **forever and ever**" (Dan. 7: 18). "They that be wise shall shine as the brightness of the firmament; and they that turn many to righteousness as the stars **forever and ever**" (Dan. 12: 3). "Him that sat on the throne, who liveth **forever and ever**" (Rev. 4: 9). "Thy throne, O God, is **forever and ever**" (Heb. 1: 8). "And there shall be no night there; and they need no candle, neither light of the sun; for the Lord God giveth them light: and they shall reign **forever and ever**" (Rev. 22: 5). "And the devil that deceived them was cast into the lake of fire and brimstone, . . . and shall be tormented day and night **forever and ever**" (Rev. 20: 10). "And he shall be tormented with fire and brimstone; . . . and the smoke of their torment ascendeth up **forever and ever:** and they have no rest day nor night" (Rev. 14: 10, 11).

As long as God shall reign, as long as his throne shall endure, as long as God shall live, and as long as the saints shall shine in the glory of the Father, the torments of the devil and wicked men will last. The Lord will live and reign "forever and ever"; and the righteous will reign with him "forever and ever." And the same Bible teaches that demons and wicked men will be tormented "forever and ever." On the strength of all these texts, which can not be broken, I affirm in the name of the God of the Bible that Scripture nowhere employs any stronger words to express the endless existence of God himself and of all that pertains to his eternal life, kingdom, and glory, than it uses to set forth both the never-ending felicities of the righteous in heaven and the never-ending torments of the wicked in hell. All who teach an ending hell are deceivers.

THERE WILL BE DEGREES OF FUTURE PUNISHMENT

This is clearly sustained by the Scriptures, and it is utterly fatal to the annihilation theory. "But after thy hardness and impenitent heart treasur-est up unto thyself wrath against the day of wrath and revelation of the right-eous judgment of God; who will render to every man according to his deeds" (Rom. 2: 5, 6). "I the Lord search the heart, I try the reins, even to give every man according to his ways, and accord-ing to the fruit of his doings" (Jer. 17: 10).

The foregoing texts apply directly to the future state, and plainly say that every man's punishment will be "ac-cording to his deeds." As there are many grades of character among the unbelieving here upon earth, so there will be many degrees of woe among the lost hereafter. "Whatsoever a man soweth, that shall he also reap." "He that soweth bountifully, shall reap also bountifully." Every act, word, and thought of our life is seed cast out on life's turbulent waters; these seeds will be swept ashore, take root, and bear a great harvest. You will reap what you sow. The more seeds of wickedness you cast out, the greater will be your harvest. "They have sown to the wind, and they reap the whirlwind." But will some have greater damnation than others? "Woe unto you, scribes and Pharisees, hypocrites! for ye devour widows' houses, and for a pretense make long prayer: therefore ye shall receive the greater damnation" (Matt. 23: 14).

Light rates the sinfulness of sin. According to the degree of light a man has, sin is sinful to him. Paul says that sin by the commandment became exceeding sinful. The knowledge of the commandment is what made sin "exceeding sinful." Jesus said to Pilate, "He that delivered me unto thee hath the **greater sin**" (John 19:11). By consenting to the wish of the Jews and condemning Christ to be crucified, Pilate committed an awful sin. Yet Christ said that the one who delivered him into Pilate's hands had the "greater sin." That was Judas Iscariot. He had more light than Pilate. Judas had once a blessed part in that sacred ministry. Because he had more light, his sin was greater. The greater the light, the deeper the sin.

"And Jesus said, For judgment I am come into this world, that they which see not might see; and that they which see might be made blind. And some of the Pharisees which were with him heard these words, and said unto him, Are we blind also? Jesus said unto them, If ye were blind, ye should have no sin: but now ye say, We see; therefore your sin remaineth" (John 9: 39-41). "If I had not come and spoken unto them, they had not had sin: but now they have no cloak for their sin. If I had not done among them the works which none other man did, they had not had sin: but now have they both seen and hated me and my Father" (John 15: 22, 24). Light, I repeat, rates the sinfulness of sin. That being true, we can easily see how men will be punished "according to their deeds," and how they must reap what they sow. Those whose sins are "exceeding sinful" because they reject greater light will receive a "greater damnation." "That servant, which knew his lord's will [had a divine revelation] and prepared not himself, . . . shall be beaten with many stripes. But he that knew not, and did commit things worthy of stripes, shall be beaten with few stripes. For unto whomsoever much is given, of him shall be much required" (Luke 12: 47, 48).

Though not only the wicked, but "all the nations that forget God" (Psa. 9: 17), will be turned into hell, yet in eternity it will be more tolerable for those nations than for the wicked wretches that willfully and knowingly went against greater light and truth. Although all will be cast into hell, conscience will doubtless be a principal part of eternal torment, and the punishment of **sense** and **separation** will be much greater to some than to others. Thus, we see not only that light rates the sinfulness of crime here, but that it will rate the punishment of the damned in hell forever. Whatever the damnation of the ungodly will be, it must and will be just (Rom. 3: 8).

"And whosoever shall not receive you, nor hear your words, when ye depart out of that house or city, shake off the dust of your feet. Verily I say unto you, It shall be more tolerable for the land of Sodom and Gomorrah in the day of judgment, than for that city" (Matt. 10: 14, 15). "Then began he to upbraid the cities wherein most of his mighty works were done, because they repented not: Woe unto thee, Chorazin! woe unto thee, Bethsaida! for if the mighty works, which were done in you, had been done in Tyre and Sidon, they would have repented long ago in sack-cloth and ashes. But I say unto you, It shall be more tolerable for Tyre and Sidon at the day of judgment, than for you. And thou, Capernaum, which art exalted unto heaven, shalt be brought down to hell: for if the mighty works, which have been done in thee, had been done in Sodom, it would have remained until this day. But I say unto you, That it shall be more tolerable for the land of Sodom in the day of judgment, than for thee" (Matt. 11: 20-24).

Jesus reproached these cities, and de-

clared that if he had done in Sodom
the same works that he did in them,
those ancient people would have repented and would not have been destroyed. He also said that in the day
of judgment the punishment of Sodom
will not be so great. If that punishment
were simply annihilation, such language
would be meaningless. Of one man,
Jesus said, "It had been good for that
man if he had never been born."

Backsliders will receive a greater
punishment than those who were never
saved. "For it had been better for them
not to have known the way of righteousness" (2 Pet. 2: 18-21). "For if we sin
wilfully after that we have received the
knowledge of the truth, there remaineth
no more sacrifice for sins, but a certain
fearful looking for of judgment and
fiery indignation, which shall devour
the adversaries. He that despised Moses'
law died without mercy under two or
three witnesses: of how much sorer pun-

ishment, suppose ye, shall he be thought
worthy, who hath trodden under foot
the Son of God, and hath counted the
blood of the covenant, wherewith he
was sanctified, an unholy thing, and
hath done despite unto the Spirit of
grace? For we know him that hath
said, Vengeance belongeth unto me, I
will recompense, saith the Lord. And
again, The Lord shall judge his people.
It is a fearful thing to fall into the hands
of the living God" (Heb. 10: 26-31).

How solemn these truths! Of all the
millions in the dark regions of despair,
the men and the women that were once
saved and then fell away from that state
will have the greatest punishment. Their
punishment will be a "much sorer punishment" than that of those who were
never saved. To all eternity they will
remember a time when they were saved
and the sweet peace of heaven filled
their souls. They will remember those
seasons of grace and glory, the sweet

hymns of Zion, the fellowship of their
Creator. They will look back to a time
when their hearts were pure, and when
they were ready to enter heaven and immortal glory. Oh, what a remembrance
for lost souls! But they sold their souls
for a feather. They bartered away the
priceless treasure of salvation for some
trifle, some of earth's vanities. Now they
are lost—eternally lost; forever cut off
from Christ and all that is pure and
lovely; sinking away farther and farther from home, heaven, and loved ones
—eternally separated. Oh, what a punishment! Yet, once they were saved. It
were better for them never to have
known the way of righteousness.

From all the foregoing texts we clearly see that men's punishment will be
"according to their deeds"; that some
will have "greater damnation," a "much
sorer punishment," than others; that
some will have "few stripes," others
"many," according to the degree of

light they have received; that it will be "more tolerable" for some than for others. This stands in direct contradiction to the doctrine of annihilation. If the ungodly will simply be burned into ashes, such scriptures have no meaning. An unconscious man, lifeless, and reduced to a bit of ashes, can not suffer.

OBJECTIONS CONSIDERED

This chapter will not be complete without considering some objections brought against the foregoing arguments by those who advocate the doctrine of annihilation. The most important one is

Death, the wages of sin.—Adventists, Russellites, and all other opposers of the Bible doctrine of endless punishment lay great stress upon the term "death." They have written books, tracts, and papers against eternal damnation, arguing that everlasting punishment is everlasting annihilation. To prove this, they freely quote all the texts that can be found stating that death is the result and wages of sin. In fact, this is their main argument. They say, "Christ paid the sinner's penalty. If that penalty is eternal torment, then Christ must suffer eternal torment. But that penalty is death, and Christ paid that penalty by dying." This may look like argument to the uninformed, and to some it appears to be unanswerable; but when viewed in the light of the Holy Spirit and eternal truth, its fallacy is easily seen. Taking their logic, what have we? The wicked will be annihilated, burned up root and branch, eternally obliterated. That is the penalty for sin. So Christ, to pay the sinner's penalty, must be annihilated, burned up, eternally obliterated.

But does not the Bible teach that the sinner shall die? Yes. "Sin, when it is finished, bringeth forth death" (Jas. 1: 14, 15). "The soul that sinneth, it

shall die" (Ezek. 18: 4). "The wages
of sin is death" (Rom. 6: 23). False
teachers merely assume the very thing
they attempt to prove, namely, that
death must necessarily mean annihilation, utter extinction of being. But such
reasoning is not according to the Bible.

Before the foregoing texts can be
wrested in defense of the annihilation
theory, three things must be proved:
(1) that they apply exclusively to the
state of the guilty beyond the judgment;
(2) that the death of a thing blots it
out of existence; (3) that the term
"death" in these texts signifies a cessation of the soul's conscious being. If
materialists can not sustain these propo-
sitions, their doctrine falls.

1. The death of the sinner is not applied exclusively to his future state, but
it is his present condition and realization.—God told Adam, "In the day that
thou eatest thereof thou shalt surely
die" (Gen. 2: 17). The penalty of

death was to fall on them, not beyond the judgment, nor thousands of years in the future, but in the very day of their sin. "In **the day** that thou eatest thereof thou shalt surely die." The devil said, "Ye shall not surely die"; and Adventists and all materialists have taken up the same falsehood, and they deny that Adam did die that day. But the divine testimony stands unbroken. On the very day that Adam transgressed the law of God, he died—not a physical death, for he lived many years after he was driven from Eden. Physical death, it is true, came upon Adam as a result of the fall (see Gen. 3: 17-19; 1 Cor. 15: 21, 22); but the sense in which he died on the day of his sin was that his soul was cut off from union with God. He died a spiritual death, became dead in sin. Sin separates the soul from God (Isa. 59: 1, 2); it cuts man off from the grace of divine life. His soul is alienated from God, and

brought under the dominion of sin.
That state of man in sin is called
"death"; and this death of the soul begins the very day sin is committed.

The soul is the volitional part of
man's being. "The fruit of my body
for the sin of my soul" (Micah 6: 7).
It is the soul which is responsible to
God. It sins, and it must be converted
—saved. "Converting the soul" (Psa.
19: 7). "The salvation of your souls"
(1 Pet. 1: 9). It is the soul of man
which receives spiritual life from God
in regeneration. "Hear, and your soul
shall live" (Isa. 55: 3).

Adam's sin not only brought him under the dominion of sin and into a state
of spiritual death, but it affected the
whole human race. "Wherefore, as by
one man sin entered into the world, and
death by sin; and so death passed upon
all men, for that all have sinned" (Rom.
5: 12). "Death by sin came upon all
men." "Death reigned from Adam to

Moses" (v. 14). Since the law could not give life (Gal. 3 : 21), death reigned from Adam until Christ. He came "that they might have life" (John 10: 10). Since Christ came, when people get saved they have "passed from death unto life" (1 John 3: 14).

So death—the state of the sinner, the wages of sin—is, in part, a present condition and state of the soul. This fact overthrows all the argument in favor of annihilation based on the word "death."

"But every man is tempted, when he is drawn away of his own lust, and enticed. Then when lust hath conceived, it bringeth forth sin: and sin, when it is finished, bringeth forth death" (Jas. 1: 14, 15). When an individual allows lust to conceive in his heart, it (lust) will bring forth death. Just as soon as a man yields to the evils of lust, he commits sin. Death is the immediate result. Hear Paul's testimony: "I was alive without the law once: but when the commandment came, sin revived, and I died" (Rom. 7: 9). The time when he was alive was during his infancy, before he had knowledge of good and evil. When he arrived at the years of accountability and obtained a knowledge of the law, or commandment, sin revived, and he died—**"I died."** The very first sin that Paul committed produced death to his soul; hence he was dead.

All sinners are "dead in trespasses and sins" (Eph. 2: 1). "Even when we were dead in sins" (v. 5). "And you, being dead in your sins" (Col. 2: 13). "He that loveth not his brother abideth in death" (1 John 3: 14). "To be carnally minded is death" (Rom. 8: 6). "Awake thou that sleepest, and arise from the dead" (Eph. 5: 14). "She that liveth in pleasure is dead while she liveth" (1 Tim. 5: 6). "Thou hast a name that thou livest, and art

dead" (Rev. 3:1). Jude speaks of
some people "twice dead, plucked up
by the roots" (Jude 12). All these
scriptures, with many more, clearly
prove that death is a present condition
of every sinner.

"The soul that sinneth, it shall die."
When? In the day that it sins. Paul
says that when he sinned, he died. Lo!
the sinner is now dead, the Bible declares. The whole unregenerated world
is in this life **abiding in death.** The
present dead state of sinners is the result of sin, a part of its wages. If they
fail to repent and obtain spiritual life,
through Jesus Christ, in this world, they
will continue in the same state of death
in the eternal world.

**2. Death does not mean annihila-
tion—utter extinction of being.**—In the
very day Adam sinned, he died (Gen.
2:17). Was he annihilated that day?
No; he lived a natural life for nine hundred and thirty years (Gen. 5:5). When

Paul came to a knowledge of God's commandment, he died—**"I died."** Was he then blotted out of existence? No; he lived to persecute the church of God and finally to preach the gospel of Christ. Multiplied scriptures teach that all sinners are now dead, abiding in death, some of them "twice dead." Are all these annihilated? No, the world is full of them; they live all around us. Yet the Bible declares they are dead. So the death of the sinner—the wages of sin—does not mean that the sinner is blotted out of existence. This fact utterly refutes and overthrows the Russellite and Adventist idea based upon the word "death"—that utter extinction of being will be the eternal portion of the impenitent.

But these teachers ask, "Can a person be dead and still living?" Yes; "she that liveth in pleasure is dead while she liveth" (1 Tim. 5: 6). Dead, yet living. The prodigal son in a far country was dead, yet was living right on (Luke 15:32). Not only is this true of the sinner here, but it will be true hereafter. If annihilation is what is meant by the second death in the lake of fire and brimstone, then all will receive the same punishment, all will be blotted out. The Bible, however, teaches that some will have "greater damnation" in hell than others; that some will receive "few stripes," others "many stripes"; that a "much sorer punishment" awaits the backslider than awaits the one who was never saved. All this proves the contrary of blotting-out. In the case of annihilation, all would receive the same doom.

Annihilation is not lasting punishment. To blot the wicked out of existence would be the opposite of "everlasting punishment," "eternal damnation," 'torment forever and ever,' which the Scriptures so plainly teach will be the eternal future of the ungodly. When the wicked are brought before the judgment-seat of Christ in "shame and everlasting contempt," and their guilty consciences lash them as they writhe beneath his piercing gaze, then to be suddenly blotted out of existence would be a speedy end to their awful punishment and would then be a glorious relief; because if they were to become unconscious, they would cease to suffer. If the wicked are to be eternally unconscious, to be no more, they would not suffer everlasting punishment, or torment, which the Bible so plainly declares they will.

Some say that the punishment of the wicked will consist in the awful thought of missing the enjoyment of heaven, and in going into utter extinction of life. If this argument be true, and the torments that they will suffer consist in such thoughts while they stand in judgment, then that torment and sense of punishment will last only until they are blotted out—just the brief moment that they stand before God. When once blotted out, they can not suffer or be tormented. Could a bit of ashes, with no consciousness, no feeling, no life, suffer? Incredible! Preposterous! But the Bible declares that the lost will be "tormented forever and ever," suffer "everlasting punishment" "in everlasting fire."

To accept the annihilation theory is to make the truth a lie. But the truth is not a lie; it will stand eternally. Again I say, to blot the wicked out of existence would bring a speedy relief instead of an everlasting punishment. Thousands in this life, suffering the pangs of a guilty conscience, have committed suicide, expecting thus to get out of misery. But such an act brings one from misery to everlasting agony and endless despair, for there is no end for the soul, a fact which we have proved by the Bible.

**3. The death of the soul, incurred
by sin, is not a cessation of the soul's
conscious existence or being.**—That
this death is the opposite of conscious
suffering, I shall prove to be utterly
false. In giving the Scriptural meaning
of the term "death" as applied to the
sinner both in this world and in that
which is to come, Webster defines it
thus: (1) "Separation or alienation of
the soul from God; a being under the
dominion of sin, and destitute of grace
and divine life; called spiritual death."
(2) "Perpetual separation from God;
and eternal torments; called the second death." These definitions exactly
express the Scriptural application of the
term "death" to the sinner, both here
and hereafter. The death of the soul
is not a cessation of its conscious being,
but an alienation from God, from his
approving smile and favor—the normal
sphere of the soul's happiness—a state
where the soul is cut off from union with

God, where it no longer partakes of his divine life. This is the wages of sin.

The death of the soul—the wages of sin—is, in part, a present condition. Every sinner, the Bible declares, is dead. Not less than one hundred clear texts prove this fact. The same state of death that the sinner is now in will be his eternal state. But is the dead sinner unconscious? is he blotted out of existence? is he annihilated? No; he lives among us; he has an existence. His soul is also conscious. It sins, and condemnation rests upon it. It is sensitive toward God. "Dead while she liveth" (1 Tim. 5: 6).

Though the sinner, as the Bible says, is now dead, yet he passes through conscious suffering—suffers remorse of conscience, suffers the guilt of his crime. This is the present experience of tens of thousands. Just so in the eternal world. As soon as a man sins, he, like Paul, dies (Rom. 7: 9). As long as he continues in sin, he "abideth in death." If such persons refuse to come to Christ that they "might have life," they will go into the eternal world dead in sin. In this world they have a chance of life; but once they pass into eternity, all chance is forever cut off, and they are doomed to suffer an eternal separation from God; doomed to abide in their present state of death.

This eternal separation from God is termed the "second death," in "a lake of fire and brimstone." But as they have a conscious existence now and suffer under the guilt of a defiled conscience, so will they in the future suffer the torments of a guilty conscience forever; and remain eternally separated from God, in that unquenchable fire where "their worm dieth not."

With the resurrection of all the dead from their graves, physical death, "the last enemy," will be destroyed (1 Cor. 15: 21-26). The state of both the righteous and the wicked beyond that day will be eternal. With physical death destroyed, the righteous will enter life eternal; and the wicked, eternal damnation, where "they have no rest day nor night," in the "mist of darkness . . . forever."

SOME ANNIHILATION ARGUMENTS CONSIDERED

Those who oppose the Bible doctrine of everlasting punishment present a number of texts of scripture that to them seem like bulwarks of truth in opposing a never-ending hell. But when such texts are critically examined and compared with the general voice of inspiration, they are found to harmonize perfectly with all the truth herein presented. Many of these texts, however, have no bearing on the subject; hence the theories built on them are but a refuge of deception, which the hail of eternal truth will sweep away. One argument against a never-ending hell is drawn from such texts as Jude 7 and 2 Pet. 2: 6. They say, "Everlasting fire will not burn forever; for eternal fire converted the cities of Sodom and Gomorrah into ashes, and now the saline waters of the Dead Sea roll over the very spot." The latter part of this statement is not recognized as a fact by standard authorities, but the argument, however, is one of the strongest used by materialists against an everlasting hell. But their deductions are false and serve to ease the guilty conscience and to soothe the sinner on the road to eternal damnation.

To sustain the foregoing proposition, they must prove that the terms "Sodom" and "Gomorrah" always refer to the houses or buildings that made up those cities. When we speak of New York and London as wicked cities, we mean the people, not the houses and buildings. Sometimes, in referring to a city or cities, we speak with exclusive reference to the streets, buildings, manufacturing plants, etc.; at other times, in referring to the same cities, we speak exclusively of the inhabitants. When the prophet said, "Behold, this was the iniquity of thy sister Sodom, pride," etc. (Ezek. 16: 49, 50), he spoke of the people. When the Lord said that it would be more tolerable for Sodom in the day of judgment than for Capernaum, he did not mean the buildings, for they had long passed out of existence, but he meant the people of that city. Yes, Sodom and Gomorrah will be at the judgment. When God rained fire and brimstone from heaven upon those ancient cities, their buildings, vegetation, and the mortal bodies of the people were turned into ashes (see 2 Pet. 2: 6). But the souls of those people of Sodom and Gomorrah, who committed fornication in "going after strange flesh," are, the apostle says, "set forth for an example, suffering the vengeance of **eternal fire**" (Jude 7)—not that the fire which literally consumed them was eternal, but that the fire of God's vengeance, which began with their literal destruction, is an eternal fire and will continue to constitute their torment.

Destroy. — Annihilationists lay no small stress on those texts which say that the wicked will be destroyed. Such scriptures as "the transgressors shall be **destroyed** together" (Psa. 37: 38), "whose end is **destruction**" (Phil. 3: 18, 19), "punished with everlasting **destruction**" (2 Thess. 1: 9), etc., are freely quoted and are considered absolute proof that the impenitent will be annihilated. That these texts, by the term "destruction," express the ultimate state and condition of the ungodly, I readily admit. But before they can be wrested in favor of the annihilation theory, it must be proved that "destroy" always means to obliterate, or blot out of existence. This, I emphatically deny.

Adventists and Russellites assume the thing that they can not prove. They say "destroy" means to blot out of existence. Sometimes it means that, but by no means does it always signify to annihilate. For example, "Egypt is **destroyed**" (Exod. 10: 7). Pharaoh's servants declared that Egypt was destroyed. The awful plagues that the Almighty sent into that land destroyed it. Yet Egypt was not blotted out of existence, annihilated; it was ruined. "The prosperity of fools shall **destroy them**" (Prov. 1: 32). Surely the prosperity of fools does not blot them out of existence. "An hypocrite with his mouth **destroyeth** his neighbor" (Prov. 11: 9). No one believes that a hypocrite with his mouth can annihilate his neighbor. A hypocrite can, however, ruin his neighbor's reputation; say things that will cast reflection on him, and thus destroy him. "A fool's mouth is his

256 CHRIST'S SECOND COMING

destruction" (Prov. 18: 7). "Be not
righteous overmuch; neither make thyself overwise: why shouldest thou **destroy thyself?"** (Eccl. 7: 16). Here are
two texts in which "destroy" and "destruction" can not mean annihilation.
Again, "My people are **destroyed** for
lack of knowledge" (Hosea 4: 6). They
ruined themselves and rendered themselves unfit for service. Not one of
them, however, was annihilated. "O
Israel, thou hast **destroyed** thyself; but
in me is thine help" (Hosea 13: 9). I
ask in all candor and reason, Did Israel
blot herself out of existence? Was
Israel as a nation annihilated? Not so.
After she had destroyed herself, God
said, "In me is thine help." Paul
preached the very faith that he once
had destroyed (Gal. 1: 23). How could
Paul preach a thing that was no more?
Ah, the very faith that Paul once destroyed was still a living faith, and he
preached it to others. Thus we could

multiply scripture texts to prove the falsity of the doctrine that teaches that "destroy" means to annihilate.

A storm may "destroy" your crops, but not "annihilate" them; a cyclone may overturn your buildings and "destroy" them, yes, leave a path of "destruction" for hundreds of miles, and yet not "annihilate" a single thing. So will sin destroy your soul, and in the day of judgment you will be sentenced to be punished with everlasting destruction in the flames of a fire that "never shall be quenched," where you will be "tormented forever and ever."

Man was created to enjoy God and to live on the plane of His nature; but when he is by sin eternally disqualified for that end, he is eternally destroyed —ruined—and will never meet the object for which he was created. He is eternally separated from communion with God,—the normal sphere of the soul's happiness. Thus he is ruined forever. Sin in this life separates between man and his God. A great chasm, or gulf, divides between them. This will be still more awfully true after souls pass into eternity; then that great gulf will be impassable (see Luke 16:19-26). Lost souls can never pass over it; they are ruined, eternally ruined.

But let us pass beyond the judgment, beyond the awful day of the Lord's coming, and what is the testimony of divine truth? "And to you who are troubled rest with us, when the Lord Jesus shall be revealed from heaven with his mighty angels, in flaming fire taking vengeance on them that know not God, and that obey not the gospel of our Lord Jesus Christ: who shall be punished with everlasting destruction from the presence of the Lord, and from the glory of his power; when he shall come to be glorified in his saints, and to be admired in all them that believe (because our testimony among you was believed) in that day" (2 Thess. 1: 7-10).

This eternal separation from God is not annihilation, as many vainly hope, but banishment "from the presence of the Lord, and from the glory of his power"; exclusion from his approbation forever, so that the light of his countenance can be no more enjoyed, as there will be an eternal impossibility of ever being reconciled to him. It is not annihilation, for their being continues; and as the destruction is everlasting, it is an eternal continuance and presence of evil and absence of all good. Thus the wicked will be eternally ruined, destroyed from the lofty end for which they were created.

Perish.—The following texts are quoted to prove utter extinction of being: "Shall utterly **perish** in their own corruption" (2 Pet. 2: 12); "Except ye repent, ye shall all likewise **perish**" (Luke 13: 1-3). That the word "perish" is here used to teach the hopeless and lost condition of the guilty, I admit; but that it teaches the doctrine of annihilation, I deny. While Webster defines the word, "To be destroyed; to become nothing," he also defines it "To incur spiritual death; to suffer spiritual or moral ruin." The latter definition conveys the Scriptural use of the word when applied to the future of the wicked. If "perish" means only to come to nothing and be no more forever, then the righteous will also be blotted out of existence eternally: "The righteous **perisheth,** and no man layeth it to heart" (Isa. 57: 1). With reference to the ungodly, the word is used to signify their hopeless and lost state in hell, where there is no hope of ever being recovered from their awful state of torment. Their hope and opportunities are forever cut off. In this sense they perish.

Consume.—There are a few texts that speak of the wicked's being consumed.

But does this mean annihilation? Listen: "We.are **consumed** by thine anger" (Psa. 90: 7). Thou "hast **consumed** us because of our iniquity" (Isa. 64: 7). 'My zeal hath **consumed** me" (Psa. 119: 139). And yet all these were still living. Thus it will be seen that such terms as "consume," "perish," "destroy," etc., in their Scriptural application, do not mean to annihilate. They express the hopeless, lost, ruined state of the wicked in their "everlasting punishment."

"Fret not thyself because of evildoers, neither be thou envious against the workers of iniquity. For they shall soon be cut down like the grass, and wither as the green herb. . . . For yet a little while, and the wicked shall not be: yea, thou shalt diligently consider his place, and it shall not be. . . . I have seen the wicked in great power, and spreading himself like a green bay-tree. Yet he passed away, and, lo, he was not: yea, I sought him, but he could not be found" (Psa. 37: 1, 2, 10, 35, 36). "For as ye have drunk upon my holy mountain, so shall all the heathen drink continually, yea, they shall drink, and they shall swallow down, and they shall be as though they had not been" (Obad. 16).

These texts are regarded as decisive in proving that the wicked will be blotted out of existence. They are quoted over and over again, and so positively that the simple and uninformed are led to believe that the texts clearly teach the opposite of everlasting punishment. False teachers find little comfort in the teachings of Christ in the New Testament. Their proof-texts are largely drawn from the Old Testament, and they are wrested from their true meaning and application, to build up erroneous theories. That the aforementioned texts prove the annihilation of the wicked beyond the great day of judgment is false. Materialists can not prove that the texts have any reference to the state of man beyond the resurrection. There is not even a hint of such a thing. Let us briefly consider each one.

In the first we are commanded not to fret because of evil-doers, nor be envious at them; "For," the psalmist assures us, "they shall soon be cut down like the grass." Does he refer to their state beyond the resurrection at the last day? No; he is speaking of natural death. "For he knoweth our frame; he remembereth that we are dust. As for man, his days are as grass: as a flower of the field, so he flourisheth. For the wind passeth over it, and it is gone; and the place thereof shall know it no more" (Psa. 103: 14-16). "Man that is born of a woman is of few days, and full of trouble. He cometh forth like a flower, and is cut down: he fleeth also as a shadow, and continueth not" (Job. 14:

1, 2). "Man that is born of a woman" "is dust," he is "of few days"; his days are "like grass"—soon cut down. This speaks of the shortness of life. Evildoers and workers of iniquity may prosper, but their prosperity lasts only a few short years. They are soon cut down by death and go hence. Does that overthrow the doctrine of eternal punishment? It has no bearing on the subject.

"Yet a little while and the wicked shall **not be.**" "I have seen the wicked in great power, and spreading himself like a green bay-tree," says the psalmist, "yet he **passed away,** and, lo, he **was not.**" And the prophet adds that the wicked is "as though he had not been." After the wicked man had passed away, David said, "I sought him, but he could not be found." When he diligently considered his place, it was not.

What weight have these poetical sayings of the psalmist's against the ever-

lasting torment of the wicked in hell?
None whatever. They have no reference to the subject. David was speaking of the folly of wickedness. He testified that he had seen wicked men
make a great display in the earth and
spread themselves like a green bay-
tree, but that they soon passed away and
were not. Death cut them down in the
midst of their great honor and prosperity, and they were no more seen on
the earth. They soon passed out of
people's memory and were "as though
they had not been." Their place in
earth's circles and societies, in the
hearts and minds of the people, could
not be found.

We all have seen the same thing—
men who for a time swept to the height
of worldly honor and drank to the full
of worldly applause, who were very
popular in the people's minds and had
a place in their hearts and affections.
Thus, like a green bay-tree, they spread

themselves; but in a few years death
cut them off. They passed away; they
were no more. Soon the memory of
them was almost forgotten. They lost
their place in the affections of the people. They are "as though they had not
been." This is precisely what the
psalmist and the prophet teach in the
texts before mentioned. To apply them
to eternity beyond the judgment, as ex-
pressing the state of the ungodly, is to
wrest Scripture out of its true meaning.

Such are the absurd wrestings of
Scripture to sustain false doctrine, resorted to by Russellites, Adventists, and
all No-Soulists. May God awaken sleeping souls ere they awaken in hell to find
their punishment just what the Bible
declares—eternal damnation.

Similar texts to the aforementioned
refer directly to death and the grave.
For example, Job 7: 9, 10: "As the
cloud is consumed and vanisheth away:
so he that goeth down to the grave shall

come up no more. He shall return no more to his house, neither shall his place know him any more." To take this text and build a theory upon it, a person might say that there will be no resurrection of the dead. The writer, however, has exclusive reference to this life and to natural death. So with all similar texts; they have no bearing on the future state of the ungodly beyond the judgment-day.

Who Is Responsible?

The prevalent teaching of our times denies eternal punishment, upon the grounds that it reflects upon the Divine character. One of the arguments used by those who oppose an everlasting hell is that it casts reflection on and detracts from the glory, the wisdom, the eternal justice, and the fatherly care and nature of God. It is also said that eternal punishment "casts reflection upon the atonement of Christ, who tasted death for every man." To the unenlightened such reasoning may seem plausible, but to those who are taught of the Lord its fallacy is obvious.

The purpose of this chapter is to show that the responsibility of man's eternal destiny rests upon man himself, and not on God. Man is responsible to God and has a free moral agency. God has not failed to make ample provision for the salvation of all mankind. He does not will that any one be lost; he wills that all be saved. He is "long-suffering to us-ward, not willing that any should perish, but that all should come to repentance" (2 Pet. 3:9). He "now commandeth all men everywhere to repent; because he hath appointed a day in the which he will judge the world in righteousness" (Acts 17:30, 31). If people spend their eternal destiny in hell, it will not be because God willed it so, but because they rejected his infinite mercy and love, and, contrary to his will, made their bed in hell. Upon whom can such cast reflection? **Upon themselves,** reason answers.

The awful calamity that befell the Jews was the result of their own disobedience and rejection of Christ. "O Jerusalem, Jerusalem, which killest the prophets, and stonest them that are sent unto thee; how often would I have gathered thy children together, as a hen doth gather her brood under her wings, and YE **would not!**" (Luke 13:34). "For thus saith the Lord God, the holy one of Israel; In returning and rest shall ye be saved; in quietness and in confidence shall be your strength: and **ye would not. But ye said, No**" (Isa. 30:15, 16). The responsibility was upon them. I would have gathered you, I would have saved you; "but ye would not"; "ye said no." Awful judgment and wrath from the Almighty came upon that people, and who was responsible? Christ laid it where it belonged —on themselves. So it will be in the day of judgment and eternity. None will then think for a moment of reflecting upon God because of their eternal destiny. It will entirely reflect upon themselves.

There are a number of reasons why this responsibility belongs to man. **Man is under law; and must pay the penalty of a broken law.** When God created the heavens, he placed all their host under certain law. The more we study the mechanism of the planetary system, the more we are convinced of the existence of the law under which they were placed. So with the earth and all its works. The vegetable kingdom, the animal kingdom—from the lowest order to the highest order—all are governed by certain laws that God has ordained. The angels, too, are under law. So when

God made man, he placed him under law.

The laws of God are "holy, just, and good." But a law without a penalty attached for its violation would be a nullity. We have state and national laws, and in order for these to be effective, certain penalties are attached for their violation. Temporal laws have temporal penalties. But the law of God under which man is placed is unlike these in that it is eternal. Being eternal in its nature, the penalty for its violation must be as eternal as the law itself. That penalty is called "death." Death means separation: spiritual death, the soul cut off from union with God; eternal death, man eternally separated from God, expressed in these words, **"Depart from me,** ye cursed, into everlasting fire." Such is the awful penalty attached to the law of God under which man is placed.

God's law is infinite. A wilful transgression of his infinite law can not but incur an infinite debt to divine justice, therefore infinite penalty or punishment is the result of transgression. The man who has committed one wilful sin against God is lost as well as the man who has committed a thousand. The law of God can not, from the nature of its author, allow the commission of a single sin. To transgress this holy law is sin; and in the language of Eliphaz, "Are not thine iniquities **infinite?**" (Job 22: 5). "How **mighty** are your sins?" (Amos 5: 12, A. S. V.).

Man has the promise of eternal felicity and a blessed union with his Maker, provided he lives in obedience to the law of his God. It is in the power of man to obey or disobey; to remain forever happy or to be eternally separated from God; to choose life or death. Man has transgressed and broken God's holy law—a just and good law. The penalty must fall upon the violator of the law. The justice and immutability of God demands the payment of penalty for crime. God can not be God and do otherwise. I ask in all candor and reason, Does this reflect upon the Lawgiver and his good law? No indeed. It reflects upon the guilty violator of the law. Who is to blame—the Lawgiver, or the violator? Reason answers, The violator. When some one openly violates the laws of our land, and as a result pays the penalty of a broken law, who is responsible? For instance, our state and national laws forbid murder. In most places the penalty is death by electricution or hanging, while in some places it is life imprisonment. When a condemned criminal is sentenced and pays the penalty for his crime, upon whom does it reflect? Who would think for a moment of reflecting upon the characters of the state and national lawmakers and the laws they have enacted? The reflection is cast upon the guilty violator of the law who is wholly responsible. Just so with the law of God. The violators of his holy, just, and good law will be wholly responsible for their eternal destiny.

And this is doubly true when we consider the fact that God has made provision whereby man can escape the awful penalty of a broken law. Mercy rejoiced against judgment, and the love of God provided an atonement in the person of Jesus Christ. "God was in Christ, reconciling the world unto himself." "Jesus Christ the righteous" became the atoning sacrifice for our sins. The stroke of justice fell on him. He suffered in our stead, "the just for the unjust, that he might bring us to God." 'He by the grace of God tasted death for every man.' Thus he satisfied divine justice and paid our penalty. What infinite love! What wondrous mercy!

Through the transgression of God's eternal law, man had contracted an in-

finite, or eternal, debt to divine justice.
He had nothing to pay. Thus he was
hopelessly, ruinously, and eternally lost.
There was but one way this infinite
debt could be removed. That was, by
pardon or forgiveness. "Forgive us our
debts." But forgiveness was made possible only through some one's satisfying
the demands of justice by paying the
debt. This is the great atonement. In
the language of the poet—

> "Jesus paid it all,
> All to him I owe."

This puts man infinitely in debt to divine mercy. God offers pardon to all
who plead guilty and confess their lost
condition.

But what of those who reject the benefits of the atonement of Christ, trample
upon his mercy, refuse to be saved, and
close their probationary state in rebellion against his throne? There can be
but one answer. They must suffer the
penalty of a broken law. To draw any

other conclusion is to cast reflection upon God. A universal salvation has been provided. A universal invitation is given. But when the majority of mankind reject these proffered mercies, refuse to accept the Christ, trample the benefits of his atonement beneath their feet, and lift their arms in rebellion against the government of heaven, and refuse to be saved, who is responsible? Every man is responsible for his eternal future. And this is no reflection on the just God of heaven.

To illustrate.—Ten men are in prison under sentence of death. They are all guilty of a certain crime. The day of execution is drawing near. But the governor issues a pardon. On a certain day the doors of the prison are unlocked, and all are invited to step out into the world free men. Two accept the invitation, while eight of them refuse, and choose to remain in prison and pay their penalty. When the day of execution arrives, and they take their place in the electric chair, upon whom can they reflect? Would they for one moment think of reflecting upon the kind governor who issued the pardon, or upon the warden who unlocked their prison cells and invited them to step out free men? No indeed. They can only reflect upon themselves for refusing the pardon and the invitation when offered. This illustrates the state of all sinners. They are in the prison-house of sin. The sentence of eternal death is hanging over all. But Christ in mercy came from heaven to earth "to proclaim liberty to the captives, and the opening of the prison to them that are bound." Some accept, but the majority reject, and choose to remain in a life of sin. They alone can be responsible.

Christ has provided salvation at a great sacrifice. He freely offers it to man. If man refuses to accept the offer, then who is responsible? To illustrate, let us suppose the people of a certain city are afflicted with a dreaded disease. As a result they are dying by the thousands. But a certain individual provides a remedy that will counteract all the effects of the disease and grant a perfect cure. He sends out a broad invitation to all the afflicted ones to come and apply his remedy. He offers it free to all. A limited few accept the invitation, apply the remedy, and are cured. Of the remainder, some curse and revile the man who offers them the cure; others scoff, jeer, and make light of the proposed remedy; still others believe the remedy to be all right, but simply neglect to apply it. When these individuals are in the throes of death, upon whom can they reflect? Would any intelligent man think for a moment of reflecting upon the kind friend who provided the remedy and offered it to them freely? Not one. The individuals themselves are wholly responsible, because they would not accept the invitation and apply the only cure at hand. This illustration clearly shows the responsibility resting on the unsaved. Sinners are morally diseased and corrupted by sin. They must, as a result, suffer the "second death," or final separation from God, in the lake which burneth with fire and brimstone. But a remedy has been provided, which is a "double cure" for sin. It is the precious blood of Christ. All are invited to come to this fountain of cleansing, and those who will accept the invitation and plunge into the crimson flood will be saved. All who refuse it will be lost. And who is responsible? Jesus said, "Ye will not come unto me, that ye might have life" (John 5: 40).

A train is bound for a certain city where a plague is raging and people are dying by the thousands. We warn the people who have boarded the train of what is before them. We exhort them to get off the train or certain destruction will befall them. But they close their ears to our warnings, and gaily ride on to certain death. When the people arrive in the city and the plague takes hold upon them, who is responsible? Can they for a moment reflect upon those who gave them warning? No indeed. They themselves are responsible. Sinners are headed for the city of destruction. They are traveling on the broad-gage road that leads there. God has given the most solemn warnings to all men that if they travel this road, certain destruction awaits them. Through the preaching of the gospel we sound out the warnings of the Almighty. But the majority of people close their ears and harden their hearts, and as a result, plunge their souls down to certain ruin. Are they not responsible? Does this reflect upon the character of God? Not in the least.

Two ways lead into eternity: a narrow way to heaven and eternal life; a broad way to hell and eternal woe. We have the power to choose which way we will travel. The Bible exhorts all men to choose the narrow way—"Choose life, that thou and thy seed may live." But the majority of people refuse to heed the exhortations given, and thus take their souls to eternal night. Are not people individually responsible?

Suppose a man is starving for food and famishing for water to quench his thirst. At great cost I provide him the necessary refreshments. I spread him a table laden with wholesome food and plenty of cool, refreshing water. I kindly invite him to sit up and partake of the same. But he refuses to eat. Time and again I come to him and kindly invite him to the table. I say, "Friend, see, I have gone to much expense to provide you nourishment that will prolong your life. Please come and partake of the same." But with curses on his lips, he drives me from him. He refuses the things I offer him, and shows no appreciation whatever for my kindness. I ask in all candor and reason, When that man dies, who is responsible? Can he reflect upon me? He has no cause whatever to do so. The reflection is all upon himself. This illustrates well the condition of the ungodly of this world. The souls of men are dying and famishing for the bread of life and for the waters of salvation. At great sacrifice, God through Christ has provided the very thing man needs. The invitation is, "Ho, every one that thirsteth, come ye to the waters, and he that hath no money; come ye, buy and eat; yea, come, buy wine and milk without money and without price." Christ says, "If any man thirst, let him come unto me and drink." And again, "I will give unto him that is athirst of the fountain of the water of life freely." But when people refuse this invitation, and choose to continue on in their desolate, sinful state, who, then, is responsible? They themselves, of course. The strongest inducements of heaven are held out to attract sinners to Christ. But people wilfully and stubbornly refuse to accept him. He is their only hope. When they meet awful punishment for rejecting the Savior, are they not accountable for that doom?

Two masters, each soliciting your service, present themselves to you. They are the Lord and the devil. You have the power to choose whom you will serve. But "to whom ye yield yourselves servants to obey, his servants ye are," and "no man can serve two masters." To serve the devil means to reap the wages of sin, which is death. To serve God is to reap the reward of the righteous, which is eternal life in the world to come. Suppose you refuse to serve God, and give your life service to the devil; can you expect to reap the reward of the righteous for service you never rendered? To illustrate: Suppose two men offer you work. Each desires your services for a year. The one has hard labor to perform and offers small wages. The other has easy work and offers good wages. You reject the latter offer and accept the former. At the end of the year to whom do you look for your wages? Of course, to the one for whom you labored. And you are responsible for the wages you get, for you chose your work and master.

Your soul is on the auction-block. You yourself are the auctioneer, and have the power to deliver it to whom you will. Before you stand two bidders: the Lord and the devil. Each wants your soul. Its value attracts their attention. The Lord has the best right to your soul, because he is "the Father of spirits," and because he created it for his glory. Not only so, but it belongs to him by purchase right. He says, "All souls are mine"; "ye are not your own; for ye are bought with a price." He purchased the souls of all men with the blood of his own Son. When you deliver your soul to the devil, you steal from God his own property. In order to get your soul, the devil offers you the glittering, fascinating things of the world; but he does not give you all he offers. In life you get disappointment, misery, woe, heartache, and sorrow. If you go to the insane asylums, the homes of the feeble-minded, the penitentiaries, the slum districts of our cities, the hell-holes of licensed saloons, the divorce courts, and wrecked homes, and behold the dissipated lives, the diseased bodies, the depressed minds, the broken hearts, the corruptions of high society, etc., you will see what the devil is today giving men for their souls. And when they come to die, his demons drag the unwilling, guilty wretches down to the caverns of everlasting night. And each individual is wholly responsible. The Lord is bidding for your soul. He offers you in life all the rich blessings of his kingdom, all things that pertain to life and godliness, joy unspeakable and full of glory, peace that passeth all understanding, "the fatness of his house," and "the rivers of his pleasures." In the hour of death, he will send his angels to bear your happy spirit to the paradise of God. In the resurrection morning, he will receive you into everlasting habitations, in his future and eternal kingdom. But if you refuse all this, remember you can not reflect upon the goodness and mercy of God, but upon yourself.

A farmer prepares his field. Two bushels of seed stand before him. One contains tares, the other wheat. He has the privilege of sowing either one, but he chooses to sow the tares. When harvest-time comes, can he expect to reap golden grain? No indeed. "Whatsoever a man soweth, that shall he also reap." And is he not responsible? You are sowing in time. You will reap in eternity. The harvest will be in proportion to the seed sown. "They have sown the wind, and they shall reap the whirlwind." Does this reflect upon God? No.

It is objected that the punishment is out of proportion to the crime. To this I reply that a sin against God is not to be compared with trespass against our fellow man. In studying the nature of sin, we must take God's view of it. The enormity of a crime is not measured by the standing of the one who commits it, but by the dignity of the one against whom it is committed. The lowest serf in the community commits the same crime and must pay the same penalty for the assassination of the ruler of his country as if a senator or congressman committed the deed. Sin stands directly opposed to holiness. The more holy a being is, the more detestable and abhorrent sin becomes. God is infinitely holy. One of his divine attributes is holiness. Hence, he is infinitely opposed to sin. The very holiness of his nature demands that all his creatures be holy. "Be ye holy, for I am holy." The holiness of his nature clothes him with majestic glory. This very glory will drive every sinner from his presence forever. Sin is rebellion against this holy, infinite God, therefore the **nature** of the crime itself is such as to require the separation of the sinner from God in time and eternity.

The regard God has for his law is shown by his opposition to the transgression of it. And this is understood by the penalty he inflicts upon the guilty sinner. The awful penalty God inflicts upon the sinner measures his opposition to sin and his view of its enormity. I quote the following forceful argument on this point from "Philosophy of the Plan of Salvation":

"Holiness signifies the purity of the divine nature from moral defilement, while justice signifies the relation which holiness causes God to sustain to men as the subjects of the divine government.
. . . .

"A lawgiver can manifest his views of the demerit of transgression in no other way than by the **penalty** which he inflicts upon the transgressor. . . . And the measure of punishment which conscience dictates is just in proportion to the opposition which the lawgiver feels to the transgression of his law, i. e., the amount of regard which he has for his own law will graduate the amount of opposition which he will feel to its transgression. The amount of opposition which any being feels to sin is in proportion to the holiness of that being, and conscience will sanction penalty up to

the amount of opposition which he feels
to crime. . . .

"The principle, then, is manifest, that
the more holy and just any being is, the
more he is opposed to sin, and the higher penalty will his conscience sanction
as the desert of transgressing the divine
law. . . . This is the foundation of penalty in the divine mind. . . . Penalty,
therefore, inflicted upon the transgressor, is the only way by which the standard of justice as it exists in the mind of
God could be revealed to men.

"The truth of this principle may be
made apparent by illustration. Suppose
a father were to express his will in relation to the government of his family,
and the regulations were no sooner
made than some of his children should
resist his authority and disobey his commands. Now, suppose the father should
not punish the offenders, but treat them
as he did his obedient children. By so
doing he would encourage the disobe-

dient, discourage the obedient, destroy his own authority, and make the impression upon the minds of all his children that he had no regard for the regulations which he had himself made. And, further, if these regulations were for the general good of the family, by not maintaining them he would convince the obedient that he did not regard their best interests, but was the friend of the rebellious. And if he were to punish for the transgression but lightly, they would suppose that he estimated but lightly a breach of his commands; and they could not, from the constitution of their minds, suppose otherwise. But if the father, when one of the children transgressed, should punish him and exclude him from favor till he submitted to his authority and acknowledged with a penitent spirit his offense, then the household would be convinced that the father's will was imperative, and that the only alternative presented to them was affectionate submission or exclusion from the society of their father and his obedient children. Thus the amount of the father's regard for his law, his interest in the well-being of his obedient children and the opposition of his nature to disobedience, would be graduated in every child's mind by the penalty which he inflicted for the transgression of his commands.

"So in the case of an absolute lawgiver: his hostility to crime could be known only by the penalty which he inflicted upon the criminal. If for the crime of theft he were to punish the offender only by the imposition of a trifling fine, the impression would be made upon every mind that he did not at heart feel much hostility to the crime of larceny. If he had the power and did not punish crime at all, he would thus reveal to the whole nation that he was in league with criminals, and himself a criminal at heart.

"So in relation to murder: if he were to let the culprit go free or inflict upon him but a slight penalty, he would thus show that his heart was tainted with guilt, and that there was no safety for good men under his government. But should he fix a penalty to transgression, declare it to all his subjects, and visit every criminal with punishment in proportion to his guilt, he would show to the world that he regarded the law, and was opposed directly and forever to its transgression.

"In like manner and in no other way could God manifest to men his infinite justice and his regard for the laws of his kingdom. Did he punish for sin with but a slight penalty, the whole universe of mind would have good reason to believe that the God of heaven was but little opposed to sin. Did he punish it with the highest degree of penalty, it would be evident to the universe that his nature was in the highest de-

gree opposed to sin and attached to
holiness. . . . The mind of man would
receive an idea of the amount of God's
opposition to sin only by the amount of
penalty which he inflicted upon the sinner."

I will close this chapter with Pollok's
description of hell, the last line of which
expresses the truth of this chapter.

HELL

"Wide was the place,
And deep as wide, and ruinous as deep.
Beneath, I saw a lake of burning fire,
With tempest tossed perpetually; and still
The waves of fiery darkness 'gainst the rocks
Of dark damnation broke, and music made
Of melancholy sort; and overhead,
And all around, wind warred with wind, storm howled
To storm, and lightning forked lightning crossed,
And thunder answered thunder, muttering sounds
Of sullen wrath; and far as sight could pierce,
Or down descend in caves of hopeless depth,
I saw most miserable beings walk,
Burning continually, yet unconsumed.
Forever wasting, yet enduring still;
Dying perpetually, yet never dead.
Some wandered lonely in the denser flames.
And some in fell encounter fiercely met,
With curses loud, and blasphemies that made
The cheek of darkness pale; and as they fought,

And cursed and gnashed their teeth, and wished to die,
Their hollow eyes did utter streams of woe.
And there were groans that ended not, and sighs
That always sighed, and tears that ever wept,
And ever fell, but not in Mercy's sight.
And Sorrow, and Repentance, and Despair
Among them walked, and to their thirsty lips
Presented frequent cups of burning gall.
And as I listened, I heard these beings curse
Almighty God, and curse the Lamb, and curse
The earth, the resurrection morn; and seek,
And ever vainly seek, for utter death.
And to their everlasting anguish still,
The thunders from above responding spoke
These words, which, through the caverns of perdition
Forlornly echoing, fell on every ear:
'Ye knew your duty, but ye did it not!' ''

The New Heaven and the New Earth

We are told in the Bible that, as "strangers and pilgrims," we are simply "sojourning here" for a time (1 Pet. 2: 11; 1: 17). This world is not our final destiny; "our citizenship is in heaven" (Phil. 3: 20). "Knowing in yourselves that ye have in heaven a better and an enduring substance." Yes, IN HEAVEN, the place of God's throne and the

home of the angels will be our eternal
home; therefore "set your affections on
things above, not on things on the
earth."

All God's people are "born from
above." Their conversation is in heav-
en. Their names "are written in heav-
en." The church of God is denominated
"the kingdom of heaven." Thus all our
hopes, our desires, and attractions are
heavenward. The mind and heart of
the Christian is naturally reaching out
unto the eternal world. Earth loses its
attraction. Its rubies and diamonds, its
silver and gold, lose their luster and
brilliancy, as the Christian, with an eye
of faith, sees his riches in heaven. "Thou
shalt have treasures in heaven." The
Christian beholds the sparkling jewels,
the unsearchable riches of Christ that
await him over there, and as he presses
forward toward the joy set before him,
earth's attractions fade away. None
but the earthly minded desire to remain

AND WHAT WILL FOLLOW

here. None but those who are void of
spiritual life desire to make this earth
their home. "Man is born for a higher
destiny than that of earth. There is a
realm where the rainbow never fades;
where the stars will be spread out before us like islands that slumber upon
the ocean; and where the beautiful beings which here pass before us like visions will stay in our presence forever."

The patriarchs and saints of the old
dispensation understood this fact and
"confessed that they were strangers and
pilgrims on the earth" (Heb. 11: 13).
They understood that this was not their
final abode. David, who reigned over
Israel and inherited the Promised Land,
says, "I am a stranger with thee, and a
sojourner, as all my fathers were" (Psa.
39: 12). They were strangers in the
earth, even in the land which they received for an inheritance—only pilgrims sojourning here for a short time.
Paul says they were seeking a country,

"a **better country,** that is, **an heavenly**"
(Heb. 11: 14, 16). All these scriptures
point us away from this earth to "another country"—yes, to a "better country," "an heavenly." Our short pil-
grimage upon earth is compared to a
handbreadth, an eagle hastening to his
prey, a swift post, a dream, a shadow,
a vapor. Time with gigantic footsteps
is bearing us to eternity. Life is soon
cut down, "and we fly away." That is,
"man goeth to his eternal home" (Eccl.
12: 5, LXX).

That eternal home is not this earth,
as the worldly minded vainly hope, but
is "a house not made with hands, **eternal in** THE HEAVENS" (2 Cor. 5: 1).
Yes, at the termination of earthly things
there remains a future inheritance
which is "eternal in the heavens"; "for
the things which are seen are temporal;
but the things which are not seen are
eternal" (2 Cor. 4: 18). Paul here
speaks of things which are "temporal"

(proskairos), for a season or time only; and then he speaks of things "eternal" (aionios), without end, as the eternal Spirit (Heb. 9:14). The things which we see with our natural eyes are only temporal. They are things which have a short duration, must have an end. "The things which are seen are temporal"—temporary, existing for a time only. The temporal things include this earth and all that pertains to it. All nature teaches this fact. The grass covers this earth with a beautiful and verdant carpet, but soon it withers and molds away. The leaves, which come forth and cheer our hearts in springtime, turn to a golden hue when the autumn winds blow, and fall to mother earth, and there decay. The sturdy oak, in whose branches the fowls of the air lodge, soon decays and is no more. The same lesson is taught in the animal kingdom. So also our mortal bodies return to dust, to mother earth. Everything

around us teaches us "the end of all
things" pertaining to earth. The earth
itself is one of the things which we see,
and Paul positively declares that all we
see is temporal—must have an end. The
eternal world, then, can not be this one
on which we now live. It is the heavenly country.

There is a place called heaven. "The
Lord he is God in heaven above" (Deut.
4:39). "The Lord's throne is in heav-
en" (Psa. 11:4). "The angels of God
in heaven" (Matt. 22:30). The Lord
Jesus Christ "was received up into heav-
en, and sat on the right hand of God"
(Mark 16:19). "Who is gone into
heaven, and is on the right hand of
God; angels and authorities and powers being made subject unto him" (1
Pet. 3:22). "For Christ is not entered
into the holy places made with hands,
which are the figures of the true; but
into **heaven itself,** now to appear in the
presence of God for us" (Heb. 9:24).

It is said of the first Christian martyr—Stephen—that he "looked stedfastly **into heaven,** and saw the glory of God, and Jesus standing on the right hand of God, and said, Behold, **I saw the heavens opened**" (Acts 7).

Yes, there is a place called heaven, and it will be our eternal home. When time has run its course; when the sun and moon have ceased to shine; when all things pertaining to earth and the earth itself have passed away and been forgotten in the dim past, then, clothed with an immortal and glorified body, we shall dwell in a building of God, a house not made with hands, "ETERNAL IN THE HEAVENS." O my soul, press forward! Pleasures forevermore await thee. O world to come, in exchange for the present! O ages, for a moment! A blessed, eternal communion in the holy, blessed, eternal life of God, in exchange for the sacrifices and sufferings of a few short years of earth. For the

joy set before me I willingly endure
hardness as a good soldier for Christ
Jesus. Yes, gladly will I forsake home
and loved ones to preach the gospel, and
in exchange receive a home in that
heavenly and better country.

Since the earth on which we now live
will have an end, what a consoling
thought to know 'in ourselves that we
have IN HEAVEN a better and an enduring substance' (Heb. 10: 34). This
enduring substance is not a literal something upon this earth, as many imagine,
but it is "an inheritance incorruptible,
and undefiled, and that fadeth not
away, reserved in heaven for you" (1
Pet. 1: 4, 5). Thus we shall have an
entrance into the "everlasting kingdom," which is "his heavenly kingdom"
(2 Pet. 1: 10, 11; 2 Tim. 4: 18). O
blessed hope! "which hope we have as
an anchor of the soul, both sure and
stedfast." My soul rests upon the promises of his Word, awaiting the hope

which is laid up for us **in heaven** (Col.
1: 5).

In view of this hope, we are instructed to lay up for ourselves "treasures in heaven" (Matt. 6: 20; Luke 12:
33; Matt. 19: 21). If this earth were
to be our eternal portion, then our treasures should be laid up here; but since it
is temporal, we are commanded to lay
up our treasures in heaven. Instead of
getting our reward on this earth, as
some teach, we shall be rewarded in
heaven. "Rejoice, and be exceeding
glad; for great is your reward **in heav-
en**" (Matt. 5: 12). "Leap for joy: for,
behold, your reward is great in heav-
en."

Jesus, speaking of that future state,
said, "In my Father's house are many
mansions: if it were not so, I would
have told you. I go to prepare a place
for you. And if I go and prepare a
place for you, I will come again, and receive you unto myself; that where I am,

there ye may be also" (John 14: 2, 3).
In the Scriptures we have "Christ's
house" and "the Father's house";
Christ's kingdom of grace here, and the
Father's kingdom of glory above. The
one applies to the earth, the other to
heaven. In the above passage Christ
speaks of our future hope. By the
"Father's house" he means heaven, for
that is the Father's dwelling-place.
Christ's house is the church here upon
earth. By entering the latter we have
access to the former, the Father's house.
By "mansions" Christ desired to impart
to the disciples that heaven, the Father's domain, is large and spacious. He
did not wish, as some people believe, to
convey the idea that everybody would
have a separate house up there; he simply resorted to language that his hear-
ers could understand. He spoke from
the standpoint of a literal building so
they could comprehend his meaning.
Since the Father's house is so spacious,

contains many mansions, "I go to prepare a place for you." Christ went into heaven (Luke 24: 51). So in heaven he is preparing our eternal home.

It may be objected that heaven has been prepared from the foundation of the world. The kingdom of heaven, or heaven itself, was prepared from the beginning of the world (Matt. 25: 34), but in that kingdom, Christ went to prepare a place for us. Again, Christ was a "Lamb slain from the foundation of the world." Yet, in reality, it was fulfilled when he came. So with the place prepared for us. In reality, Christ went to prepare it for us; and the promise is that he will come again, not to remain here upon earth with us, but to receive us to himself, that where he is there we may be also; that is, he will come back and take his church home to glory, to the world he went to prepare.

When will all this be fulfilled? "For the Lord himself shall descend from heaven with a shout, with the voice of the archangel, and with the trump of God: and the dead in Christ shall rise first: then we which are alive and remain shall be caught up together with them in the clouds, to meet the Lord in the air: and so shall we ever be with the Lord" (1 Thess. 4: 16, 17). Oh, the beauty of heavenly truth! The church ʋame out of heaven, and at last it will all be caught up to heaven and be ever with the Lord.

"But," says one, "did not Jesus teach that the meek 'shall inherit the earth' (Matt. 5: 5)? The Psalmist adds, 'But the meek shall inherit the earth' (Psa. 37: 11). How harmonize 1 Thess. 4: 16, 17, with these scriptures?" Peter fully explains them. He first shows that in the day of judgment this terrestrial globe, this earth, will pass away by being burned up. He foretells its utter destruction: "But the day of the Lord will come as a thief in the night; in the which the heavens shall pass away with a great noise, and the elements shall melt with fervent heat, the earth also and the works that are therein shall be burned up" (2 Pet. 3: 10). "What, then, about the promise of Jesus, that the meek shall inherit the earth?" The apostle answers, "We, according to his promise, **look for new heavens and a new earth**" (v. 13). How clear! "We, according to his promise, look for new heavens, and a new earth," after the heavens and the earth that compose this globe are "burned up" and "pass away" (2 Pet. 3: 7-13). Peter is speaking of that land of light and bliss which Jesus went to prepare.

Also, the Revelator, after describing the judgment-scene, when this earth and its heavens fled away, "and there was found no place for them" (Rev. 20: 11-15), says, "I saw a new heaven and a new earth: for the first heaven and the first earth were passed away! and

there was no more sea" (Rev. 21:1).
He saw the new heaven and the new
earth after "the first heaven and the
first earth were passed away." So,
then, after this earth has passed away,
we look for **new heavens and a new
earth** (v. 13). The new earth is the
"heavenly country," the "better country" (Heb. 11:16).

The new heavens and the new earth
will be so much grander than this, that
the present heavens and earth "shall
not be remembered, nor come into
mind" (Isa. 65:17); and, unlike the
present heavens and earth, which shall
pass away, the new heavens and new
earth "shall remain" (Isa. 66:22).

The Golden City

In the Book of Revelation there are
given several series of prophecy that
cover the events of the Christian era

in their relationship to the church of God. Each of these series ends with a termination of the powers of wickedness and their complete overthrow. Only in one of these series is the final reward of the redeemed brought to view, and that is but briefly referred to in the closing verses of chapter 7. The last and final of these series in this wonderful book of symbols, we have in chapter 20. It ends with the coming of Christ upon the great white throne of judgment, with the passing away of the present heavens and earth, which compose this world upon which we live, the universal resurrection of all the dead, the final separation of the righteous and the wicked, and the casting into the lake of fire of all whose names were not found written in the book of life.

With the opening of chapter 21, the climax of the entire book of symbols is reached in the final and eternal reward of the redeemed. The church, having

passed through so many conflicts and
battles, is seen at last in triumphant
reign in the new heaven and the new
earth, dwelling in the golden city, which
is a fit symbol of our future and eternal
abode. Of course, to give a perfect description of heaven itself, and convey
the same to the finite mind, is not possible. But by the new heaven and the
new earth and the golden city, the Lord
has given us at least an idea of the
things which he has prepared for them
that love him. Not only is heaven
spoken of as a better **country,** a new
earth, but as a **city.** "For here have we
no continuing city, but **we seek one to
come"** (Heb. 13: 14). Yea, God hath
prepared for us **a city** (Heb. 11: 16).
In Revelation 21 this city is called "the
holy city, new Jerusalem." Because
the church on earth is properly the
depository of all the rich blessings and
graces of heaven itself, representing the
kingdom of heaven among men, it is

sometimes referred to as "Jerusalem from above," "the heavenly Jerusalem," etc. But the city brought to view in Revelation 21 and 22 is located in the new earth after the present earth has passed away. It appears after the resurrection and judgment. Only those whose names are in the Lamb's book of life will be admitted into that city (Rev. 21: 27). "Blessed are they that do his commandments, that they may have right to the tree of life, and may enter in through the gates into the city" (Rev. 22: 14). These texts make clear that the entering into this city is future.

"God himself shall be with them, and be their God. And God shall wipe away all tears from their eyes; and there shall be no more death, neither sorrow, nor crying, neither shall there be any more pain: for the former things are passed away" (Rev. 21: 3, 4). "And they shall see his face; and his name shall be in their foreheads" (22: 4).

What a beautiful description of the
glories of that eternal state. Surely the
sufferings of the present time are not
to compare with the glory that shall be
revealed. "I will give to him that is
athirst of the fountain of the water of
life freely" (21: 6). There the over-
comers "shall inherit all things" (v. 7).
"And he showed me a pure river of
water of life clear as crystal, proceeding
out of the throne of God and of the
Lamb" (22: 1). John saw this city as
"having the glory of God: and her light
was like unto a stone most precious,
even like a jasper stone, clear as crystal" (21: 11). "And I saw no temple
therein; for the Lord God Almighty and
the Lamb are the temple of it. And the
city hath no need of the sun, neither of
the moon, to shine in it: for the glory
of God did lighten it, and the Lamb is
the light thereof. And the nations of
them which are saved shall walk in the
light of it. . . . for there shall be no

night there" (vs. 22-25). "And there shall be no night there; and they need no candle, neither light of the sun; for the Lord God giveth them light: and they shall reign forever and ever" (22: 5). "And the building of the wall of it was of jasper: and the city was pure gold, like unto clear glass. And the foundations of the wall were garnished with all manner of precious stones." "And the twelve gates were twelve pearls; every several gate was of one pearl; and the street of the city was pure gold, as it were transparent glass." "And he that sat upon the throne said, Behold, I make all things new." This is the new heavens and the new earth.

In this golden city of the new earth the King of heaven will have his throne and reign forever and ever. Here the righteous shall "shine forth as the sun in the kingdom of their Father," yea, "as the stars for ever and ever."

Eternity

In Isa. 57: 15, it is said that God "inhabiteth eternity." This is the only text in the Bible where the word "eternity" occurs. It is one of the greatest and most comprehensive words in any language. In life, we are the subjects of Time. We are told, however, that the day is approaching when an angel shall swear by him that liveth for ever and ever that there shall be time no longer (Rev. 10: 6). This means eternity.

Time has a beginning and an ending. It is a fragment of eternity. It might be likened to a small island in the midst of the ocean. Gradually its sands are washed away by the mighty billows which sweep against its shores. By degrees, it is being washed away, until at length, God only knows how soon, the billows of eternity will sweep over and wash away the last sands of time, and nothing will remain but eternity.

Time is a measured portion of duration. Moments, hours, days, weeks, months, years, centuries, and ages, measure time. But eternity! No cycle of years can measure it. It is a boundless ocean, a shoreless sea, or as Paul expresses it, a "world without end." It is without beginning or ending. It takes ten hundred thousand years to make a million, a thousand million to make a billion, a thousand billion to make a trillion, a thousand trillion to make a quadrillion, a thousand quadrillion to make a quintillion, a thousand quintillion to make a sextillion, a thousand sextillion to make a septillion, a thousand septillion to make an octillion, a thousand octillion to make a nonillion, a thousand nonillion to make a decillion (1,000,000,000,000,000,000,-000,000,000,000,000). But this vast number does not express eternity.

Let us suppose that a bird comes from a far distant planet, making one trip in each decillion years. It carries away as much water in its tiny mouth as it can contain. The length of time required by that bird to thus transfer to the distant planet all the waters contained in the springs, rivers, lakes, and oceans, would not measure eternity. After carrying away all the waters suppose the bird still continues its journeys to earth, coming but once in a decillion of years, and carries away in its tiny mouth a grain of sand from the seashore, or a bit of dust. That bird could carry away the entire globe on which we live, and yet eternity would not be measured.

Dear reader, you are going to eternity. We all shall soon be there. Death is the gateway each of us must pass through, and death fixes our destiny either in heaven or in hell. You are now forming a character for eternity. You are sowing seed, the harvest of which you must there reap. Now is the only time to prepare.   There are three terms which express eternity. They are: **everlasting, eternal,** and **forever and ever.** All these terms are used to convey to our minds the duration of the felicities of the righteous in heaven and the torment and punishment of the wicked in hell.   We are all travelers to eternity, whether saved or unsaved. We must all spend eternity somewhere. The righteous, amid the glories of the new heaven and earth; the wicked, amid the horrors of a never-ending night.   In view of this solemn fact, as a final exhortation, I say to all in the language of the prophet, "PREPARE TO MEET THY GOD."

THE END